REVELATION:
Book of Mystery and Hope

Revelation

BOOK
OF MYSTERY
AND HOPE

C. E. COLTON

BROADMAN PRESS
Nashville, Tennessee

4213-84

ISBN: 0-8054-1384-7

Dewey Decimal Classification: 228

Subject heading: BIBLE.   N. T.   REVELATION

Library of Congress Catalog Card Number: 79-52981

Printed in the United States of America

PREFACE

My investigative passions toward this last book in our divine library were first stimulated while listening to my seminary teacher, Dr. H. E. Dana, as he shared with his students his insights into this book of mystery and hope. His approach to the book of Revelation made sense to me, and this is the basic approach I have maintained through the years. As one reads through this volume, he will detect the influence of Dr. Dana if he is familiar with his exposition of the Apocalypse.[1]

This is not a verse-by-verse exposition. I have tried to set out what I believe to be the basic and practical teachings of this last book in our Bible. Many of the details have been passed over rather lightly in order to make it more readable and attractive to the average lay person. The reader will find it advantageous to have his Bible open before him as he studies this book. In fact, I would recommend a fresh reading or rereading of the Bible book before turning through the pages of this book.

I am aware of the fact that not all readers of this book will agree with the interpretation given herein. Perhaps there is no book in the Bible concerning which there is a wider range of interpretations. Even though the reader may not agree with the details of this interpretation, I trust that he will find fresh courage and hope as he envisions with John the glorious consummate victory of Christ and his kingdom. Regardless of our differences of opinion as to the methods and the chronology of events, all who know Christ through a personal experience of regeneration will surely agree that the time will come when "The kingdoms of this world are become the kingdoms of our Lord, and of his Christ; and he shall reign for ever and ever" (11:15).

I am indebted to many people who have helped me in my study of the Apocalypse and the preparation of this book. Many of those who have helped me through their published works are recognized in the footnotes at the end of the book. These will suffice to give the reader a limited bibliography should he desire to do further study in this area. I would like to register public acknowledgment and appreciation to Paul Moore, a fellow staff member, who read the manuscript and made valuable suggestions and corrections, and to my son, Robert E. Colton, for helpful suggestions concerning literary forms and grammatical constructions.

May the Lord bless this volume as it falls into the hands of those who may need the encouragement and stimulation which God has designed to give through these visions which have been relayed to us through his servant John.

C. E. COLTON

Dallas, Texas

CONTENTS

CHAPTER ONE
Introduction

The book of Revelation introduces itself in its first three verses thusly: "The Revelation of Jesus Christ, which God gave unto him, to shew unto his servants things which must shortly come to pass; and he sent and signified it by his angel unto his servant John: / Who bare record of the word of God, and of th testimony of Jesus Christ, and of all things that he saw. / Blessed is he that readeth, and they that hear the words of this prophecy, and keep those things which are written therein: for the time is at hand" (1:1-3).

These three verses constitute somewhat of a subtitle to the book. In fact, in its original form it was the only title. This title sets forth the nature and purpose of the book. It is "The Revelation of Jesus Christ." Some prefer to use a transliteration of the Greek word, Apocalypse, which means to uncover something which has been covered up. It is not a "covering up" or a "hiding," as some seem to think. It is a revealing, the unveiling of some things which have hitherto been unknown.

This revelation, John tells us, is "of Jesus Christ." There are two ways to interpret this clarifying phrase. If the genitive is objective, the picture about to be unveiled is a revealing of Christ or a showing forth of Christ. If the genitive is subjective, the picture is one that Christ has given. Either of these is grammatically possible. Certainly it is Jesus Christ who stands in the forefront of the picture which is about to be unveiled; but the clause which follows, "which God gave unto him," seems to indicate the subjective idea. It is a revelation which Christ is giving. God gave it to Christ; and he, in turn, gave it to the angel, who conveyed it to John.

There is a sense in which both ideas are true, and it would be useless to quibble over this detail. Some preachers take the genitive here to be objective and explain that this portrait revealing Christ is what God has given to his Son as a reward for his part in the redemptive plan.[1] This may be taking the implications of the text a little too far, though it is not impossible. It seems more natural to make the genitive subjective. This would mean that the Revelation is an unveiling which is about to be made by Jesus Christ through the angel to John. It will involve Jesus Christ himself, of course; but it will also involve "things which must shortly come to pass."

We are told very plainly that the human author is a man named John, but we still have the problem of determining which John. There are some five or six different men who went by this name in the New Testament. Most of the scholars agree that this book was written by the same man who wrote the Gospel and the Epistles of John, though there are some who vigorously disagree, such as A. M. Hunter and others.[2] These dissenting scholars do not have any conclusive opinion as to the identity of the author, but they are quite sure that the apostle John did not write it. It would be useless to delve into all the minute details of these arguments. Suffice it to say that there are some recognizable differences in terminology and style, but in my opinion not enough to merit the conclusion drawn by A. M. Hunter. There are far more similarities than differences, and the differences are reasonably explained by differences in time, environment, and nature of the subject matter. So far as I am concerned, the author of the Revelation was none other than John the apostle, the one who leaned on Jesus' bosom at the Last Supper and the one who wrote the Gospel and Epistles bearing his name. The important thing for us to remember is that God used a man by the name of John through whom to bring to us this marvelous unveiling.

It will be helpful if we can learn something of the identity and circumstances of the original readers. We do have some definite clues on this subject. John tells us in the fourth verse that he is addressing this message to "the seven churches which are in Asia." Presently he identifies those churches as Ephesus, Smyrna, Pergamos, Thyatira, Sardis, Philadelphia, and Laodicea. Obviously the message is intended for the Christians who are identified with these churches. Generalizing still further, we may safely assume that the original readers were the Christians of Asia Minor.

So far so good, but what can we learn as to the time and circumstances which prevailed when John wrote to them? This question is not so easily answered, but we believe that there are some rather distinct implications. Though it cannot be proved beyond any shadow of doubt, most of the scholars believe that John wrote this book during the time of the Domitian persecutions, between A.D. 90 and 100. There are several factors which seem to point to this conclusion, not the least of which is the fact that John's descriptions of conditions seem to fit into the pattern of what we know of Domitian's reign. These will be brought out more clearly as we proceed in our exposition of the book.

If this be true, and we have good reason to believe that it is, we can understand a little better the circumstances which prevailed among the Christians of Asia Minor at the time John wrote. Throughout the Roman Empire, Domitian decreed that all men must worship the emperor and his image. Those who refused were imprisoned or beaten, and some were martyred. It was a dreadful day for Christianity. John himself had been exiled to the desolate Isle of Patmos because he preached the gospel of submission to the Lord Jesus, who was considered by the officials as a rival to the emperor. John had labored long with these beloved Christians of Asia Minor, but now he had been taken away from them; and they never knew at what moment the government agent would come to depose another Christian. For all they knew, John was dead. Their hearts were deeply grieved at this turn of events.

Christians had to meet behind closed doors. They lived in constant fear of being brought before one of the officials. In many cases property was confiscated by the government. Under such conditions the Christians were weary, despondent, and discouraged. They could see nothing but the rise of satanic might. They had begun to wonder if the cause of Christ had been utterly lost. It was a most trying hour. Though John wrote to Christians of the first century under such circumstances as described above, the message of this book is especially appropriate for Christians of any era who suffer persecution and are discouraged. If the time should come, and it surely will, that Christians will be subjected again to merciless persecutions at the hands of godless dictators, then the book of Revelation will take on new meaning and significance. For those who truly love the Lord it is always precious and fascinating.

John had one primary purpose in mind when he wrote the Apocalypse—to encourage and strengthen the faith of these buffeted and discouraged Christians of Asia Minor, and any others down through the years who would be called upon to endure such sufferings. If we lose sight of this purpose, we will miss the true meaning of the book. In order to encourage the disheartened disciples, John was privileged by the inspiration of the

Holy Spirit to show them the unfolding of God's redemptive program, revealing its glorious and complete triumph for the redeemed of God and the utter destruction of all the forces of evil.

The theme of the book thus appears. Let us never lose sight of it. It is the story of redemption with emphasis upon its glorious consummation. In the expositions which follow, we will have occasion to watch this blessed story unfold. At this point we shall give only a general preview to show the makeup of the drama and its main divisions.

The main body of the book begins with the fourth chapter. The first three chapters constitute an introduction or preparation for the main message. In true first-century epistolary form, the letter begins with a salutation (1:4-9), which includes an identity of the writer and the readers, with a warm Christian greeting involving all three persons of the Trinity.

Verse 10 introduces us to a preliminary vision of Christ steeped in significant symbolism. This vision was designed to prepare his readers for the symbolic nature of the message which he is about to give to them. It is important, not only as a revelation of Christ, but also as a clue to the nature of the book.

Chapters 2 and 3 contain seven brief, practical letters to seven churches. These also are designed to prepare the people for the main body of the revelation while giving some practical exhortations for daily living.

The main body of the book, as to its basic structure, has been variously viewed by the different scholars; but it seems to me that the book falls rather naturally into seven main divisions as follows:

• a picture of sovereignty and majesty with God on his throne and the lamb by his side (4:1 to 5:14)

• a picture of righteous judgment (6:1 to 8:5)

• a picture of timely and forceful warning (8:6 to 11:19)

• a picture of the inevitable conflict between the forces of evil and the forces of righteousness (12:1 to 15:8)

• a picture of the climax of the conflict (16)

• a picture of the celebration of victory (17:1 to 20:10)

• a picture of eternal destiny (20:11 to 22:5)

• an epilogue (22:6-21)

One's general attitude toward the book of Revelation is a vital factor in one's interpretation of the book. Generally speaking, there are four attitudes which various scholars have taken in their approach to this last book of the Bible. Some have taken what is known as the preterist attitude. A preterist in theology is one who thinks of all prophecy as that which has already come to pass. He, therefore, looks upon the book of Revelation as a series of oracles or events having only historical significance. To him the book of Revelation has nothing to say about the present or the future. It is simply a historical document which refers to the Christians of the first century. It tells us what

they did and what they thought. It is interesting
and valuable from the standpoint of history, but
has no real pertinent value for the present-day
Christian, except as it describes conditions which
may be similar to some of our own.

Others assume the attitude that in the book of
Revelation we have a panoramic view of world
history, or, to be more exact, Christian history.
These are they who find a prophetic reference to
every major event in history, plus the events which
are yet to be, right on up to the final consummation. This is sometimes referred to as the continu-
ous-historical method of interpreting the book of
Revelation. People with this attitude see in the
seven churches of Asia seven distinct eras in
Christian history which are further explained in
the seven main divisions of the book. Some distin-
guished and highly regarded scholars may be classified in this category, such as John Wycliffe, Mar-
tin Luther, Albert Barnes,[3] and B. H. Carroll.[4]

All who assume this attitude seek to interpret
every part of the Apocalypse so as to fit into this
general idea of church history. In this camp will
be found most of those who hold the postmillen-
nial position concerning eschatology. This is not
to say that all in this camp are postmillennialists,
but it does mean that most postmillennialists will
be found here. We simply mention this in passing.
The various millennial positions will be discussed
in detail when we come to the twentieth chapter
of the Revelation.

Then there is the futurist attitude. Proponents

of this attitude are rather numerous, especially in the twentieth century. Those who assume this attitude take the position that everything in the book of Revelation, that is, in the main body (chaps. 4—22), refers to that which is yet future, in particular to that which will come to pass immediately before the second coming of Christ. This attitude is rather popular in our day and is espoused by some very capable and respectable Bible scholars, such as J. N. Darby, C. I. Scofield,[5], George Ladd,[6] W. A. Criswell,[7] J. Dwight Pentecost,[8] and John Walvoord.[9]

While there may be rather wide differences of opinions on the details, all of these regard the book of Revelation as wholly eschatological. In fact, most of them hold that the events from chapters 4—19 are to take place within the brief space of seven years immediately preceding the final return of Christ. However, there are differences of opinion as to whether or not the Christians will be involved in these seven years of tribulation. Some say that the Christians will be raptured away before the tribulation; others, at the midpoint; and still others, after it. Most of the futurists insist on a very literal interpretation of the book all the way through. Albertus Pieters divides all futurists into two schools: those who hold to a strict dispensational view and those who make no distinction between the "rapture" and the "revelation." [10] Actually, there are many variations of interpretation among the futurists, but all of them are agreed on the idea that the book of

Revelation speaks only of the future endtime, and most of them would be classified as premillennialists.

A fourth attitude is that which looks upon the book of Revelation as a purely symbolic representation of the philosophy of history. These are they who see no particular events as such portrayed in the book, but they do see certain basic principles of Christian history expressed in symbolic form. They look upon the book as purely symbolic or figurative. This is not to say that it has no historic basis, for they do recognize that the book grew out of certain historic circumstances which existed in the first century; but they do not see a schedule of events either past, present, or future. What they do see is a presentation in symbolic form of certain basic principles which are operative in redemptive history whether past, present, or future. The element of time has little significance in this approach to the book. As in the other positions, there are variations of viewpoint; but the basic idea is that of looking for principles, such as causes, effects, and motives, rather than programs and schedules of events. Outstanding scholars are also to be found in this category, such as J. Gresham Machen,[11] H. E. Dana,[12] Ray Summers,[13] David Freeman,[14] and Albertus Pieters.[15] In relation to eschatology, most of the scholars in this category would be classified as amillennialists, though the term has been often misunderstood and misinterpreted. This, too, will be explained in further detail when we come to Revelation 20.

While these are the four basic attitudes toward the book of Revelation, there is still another attitude which is somewhat of a synthesis of these four. It is the attitude I have assumed in this study. I have sought diligently to classify myself in the light of these four basic attitudes and find it extremely difficult to put myself in any one of the four positions. I have found some acceptable elements in each of the four positions and have sought to blend these into my own attitude toward the book. In the strictest sense I am neither a premillennialist, a postmillennialist, or an amillennialist. I agree with the first position in that I see a real historic basis for the Revelation. I agree with the second position in that I see the basic patterns for the unfolding of Christian history, since history does repeat itself from era to era. I agree with the futurist in that I see that some parts of the Revelation do refer to the future and the future only. But I also agree with the fourth position in that I see the basic factors or principles in the unfolding of God's redemptive plan. Perhaps this attitude is more predominant than the others; yet some aspects of the interpretations given in this study will not fit into any of these categories, in particular our interpretation of the millennial question.

Regardless of one's basic attitude toward the book of Revelation, there are two extreme positions which ought to be avoided by the sincere Bible student. First, he should avoid the attitude of assuming too much dogmatic certainty concerning every detail. There are those who seem to know beyond any shadow of doubt exactly what every symbol means, and they insist that theirs is the only right answer. In a book so completely saturated with figurative language, no one can afford to be dogmatically certain about every detail. The basic ideas and the primary thoughts running through the book are clear enough; but if one is honest, he will have to confess that there are a number of enigmas in the book concerning which he cannot be dogmatic. Beware of that Bible teacher who claims to have the final and authoritative answer to every detail in the book of Revelation. He may impress some people as one who is highly intelligent and spiritually enlightened, but a careful examination will usually reveal that he is shallow and presumptuous. Avoid him like a plague.

The other extreme position is just as dangerous—that of looking upon the book of Revelation as some kind of a sacred but mysterious book which was never intended to be understood. Therefore, it should be left upon the table untouched. This is the attitude assumed by too many Christians of our day. To them the Revelation is a mysterious untouchable and beyond human comprehension. It is too sacred to touch. But God never intended for any Christian to take this attitude toward this last book of our Bible. Let us remember that Revelation is an uncovering, not a covering up. There is a message in it for all of God's people, and we can find that message if we seek for it through diligent study under the guidance of the Holy Spirit. Some of the details shall forever remain indistinct, but the basic message is there for all who really want it. Let us approach our study of this book with the assurance that God does have a message in it for us. And we can understand that message, at least in its basic outline, if we seek it prayerfully and sincerely.

CHAPTER TWO
The Format of the Apocalypse

Continuing in the area of introduction, let us take a closer look at the nature of the format of the book. Even a cursory reading will convince the student that this book is different in style from any other book of the New Testament. The whole message is couched in figures, symbols, and weird images.

These symbols appear in many different forms. Some of them are taken from animate life and some from inanimate life. Here are a few of the more frequently used symbols found in the book: beast (twenty-two times), seal (seventeen times), dragon (fourteen times), book (twenty-five times), lamb (twenty-eight times), throne (twenty-two times), living creatures (fourteen times), trumpet (five times), the number seven (fifty-seven times), the number three and one-half (seven times), the number twelve (ten times), and the number four (ten times). Besides these more familiar symbols, there are many others such as frogs, locusts, scorpions, lions, a scarlet woman, candlesticks, and all sorts of mystic figures.

If John wrote to encourage the disheartened and

persecuted Christians of Asia Minor by showing them the ultimate triumph of Christ and his redeemed people, why did he not say it in plain language? Why did he have to couch his message in such strange and sometimes weird figures? Why must the message be blurred by these strange figures of speech? These are doubtless the first questions to come into the mind of the average reader of the Apocalypse.

There is a reasonable answer to these questions. One thing is sure—John did not write in symbols in order to confuse the intended readers. Nor was it because John did not know how to write in plain and simple language. One glance at the Gospel of John or one of his letters will be sufficient to prove John's ability to write in simple and understandable language.

But why, some will ask, did he not write the Revelation in the same format as he did his Gospel and his epistles? Why must this one be so different? There are two good reasons. First, John had to write this letter in terms of figures and symbols because it was the only way that he could have gotten the message to its intended readers. Let us remember that John wrote this letter during a time of severe persecution and under a government which was antagonistic to the gospel. John himself, at the time he wrote this letter, was a prisoner of that hostile government. He had been exiled to the lonely Isle of Patmos off the coast of Asia Minor in the Aegean Sea. He had been arrested because he preached submission to a

"foreign ruler," Jesus Christ. In the minds of the
Roman officials, Jesus Christ was a rival to the
throne of the emperor. John perhaps would have
been executed on the spot, as were some others,
except for the fact that he was already an old
man; therefore, the authorities "graciously" allowed him to live out his last few months or years
on the desolate Isle of Patmos.

Patmos is about forty miles off the coast of Mile-
tus. It had been used for some time by the Roman
government as a place of punishment and safe-
keeping for prisoners. It was a lonely and desolate
island, with only a few rock quarries where the
prisoners were compelled to work. A ship would
dock on the island once in a while to pick up a
cargo of rock. Otherwise, it was a quiet and lonely
place. This made it possible for the aged apostle
to have ample time for meditation, prayer, and
reflection. It was on this forsaken island that God
gave to John this glorious message concerning the
triumphant consummation of our redemption.

The message itself was clear enough, but John's
problem was that of getting the message through
to those buffeted and suffering Christians of Asia
Minor. God gave him the answer in the form of
a vision, which John simply recorded as he saw
it and sent it on to the suffering Christians of Asia
Minor. Had he written out the message in plain
language, it would have been intercepted by the
Roman censors and destroyed along with its author, especially that part of it which had to do
with the downfall of the wicked empire. Some of

the symbols and figures John was able to explain to his readers, but others could not be so interpreted without serious consequences. Perhaps his readers did not decipher every detail of the symbols, but they were doubtless able to interpret and understand the overall message. It was a message to Christian friends written in code language in order to escape the severe and treacherous hand of a hostile emperor. We may well imagine that when the Roman censors came to this letter of John's to his friends in Asia Minor, they considered it to be nothing more than meaningless jargon coming from an old man with a delirious mind. I can almost hear one of them say to another: "That poor old man, John! He has just about lost his mind. This letter is nothing but meaningless nonsense. It surely can do no harm. Let it go through."

Because of the dangers which confronted Christians from a hostile government, it is very likely that some of these symbols had been reviewed before John was taken away. Others were symbols which had been known to all Jews for centuries. Literature written in this form has come to be known as apocalyptic literature. There are three books in our Bible which make much use of such symbols and figures: Ezekiel, Daniel, and the Revelation. All three were written during a period of foreign or hostile reign. Ezekiel and Daniel were written during the time of the Jewish captivity. Both lived under the reign of a foreign power. When they spoke of the downfall of the reigning monarch or monarchy, they, like John, had to

speak in code language. In his discussion of the
nature of apocalyptic literature, Dr. Ray Summers
makes this interesting comment:

> It is readily seen that troublous times gave
> birth to apocalyptic literature. Trial, suffering,
> sorrow, and near-despair furnished the soil in
> which this type of writing grew. Written in days
> of adversity, this form of expression always
> set forth the present as a time of great persecu-
> tion and suffering, but, in glorious contrast, the
> future as a time of deliverance and triumph.[1]

Dr. Summers also points out four characteristics
of apocalyptic literature which should always be
taken into consideration by the reader: (1) It always possesses a historical significance; (2) Generally it is of pseudonymous authorship (even
though the name John is used in the Revelation,
it is not clearly identified); (3) It makes much use
of visions; (4) It makes much use of the symbol.

But there is also a second reason for John's use
of the symbolic and figurative. He was describing
heavenly things as seen from heaven's point of
view. John was faced with the task of trying to
describe the indescribable. The realities of the
spirit and future world can only be described in
concrete language for the man who lives in this
world. The human language and the human mind
are utterly incapable of comprehending or describing that which is heavenly. The best we can do
is to use a symbol which may suggest to the mind
certain spiritual ideas. Even then our understanding is imperfect, but it is the only way by which

we can approximate it. When John began to talk about the things of this world as they are seen from the other world, he could only use terms or symbols with which his readers were familiar. Only in this way could we grasp even a partial understanding of what it will be like when we are able to view it from the other side.

In the light of what we have just said, we must understand that the symbols are but vehicles to convey spiritual truths. Therefore, it is both unreasonable and dangerous to insist on a literal interpretation of these symbols. It is at this point that some have sadly abused this last book in our Bible. There are those who insist that we must always give a literal interpretation to the Scriptures in every part of the Bible; yet these same people frequently break this rule which they set up for themselves. There is absolutely nobody who gives a literal interpretation to every word in the Bible. For instance, I know of no one who gives a literal interpretation to the words of Jesus which he uttered in his Sermon on the Mount, "Ye are the salt of the earth" (Matt. 5:13). Everyone knows that this is symbolic language and was never intended to be interpreted literally. It would be utterly ridiculous to conclude that Jesus meant to say that the Christian is a literal block of salt. The Bible uses many such metaphors and analogies, and the whole of the book of Revelation is couched in figurative language. Much of the Bible is to be taken literally, but there are instances in which the symbolic use of a word is obvious.

In a highly figurative book such as the Revelation, the literalist must break his own rule many times. Even the most avid literalist interprets some of the terms in the Revelation figuratively. For instance, I know of no Bible scholar who thinks that there literally will be three slick, slimy frogs who will come forth to rally an army to fight against the people of God; yet some of these same scholars will demand that we must give a literal meaning to other terms which are just as obviously figurative. Such scholars may be classified as hyperliteralists. They insist on a literal interpretation of only certain verses of Scripture in order to justify some preconceived supposition. Then they proceed to criticize those who "spiritualize" the Scripture while they themselves do the same thing with reference to other Scriptures.

A good example of this inconsistency may be found in Dr. John Walvoord's book *The Millennial Kingdom*. He strongly criticizes those who "spiritualize" in their interpretation of the Revelation; yet he himself confesses that "obvious figurative language or instances where the New Testament gives authority for interpreting the Old Testament in other than a literal sense would be just grounds for use of the spiritualizing method. Obviously, some Scriptures of the Old Testament and a few passages of the New Testament have a figurative meaning." [2]

The advice of Floyd Hamilton is well worth following as we approach our study of the Revelation:

> The literal interpretation of the prophecy is to be accepted unless (a) the passages contain obviously figurative language, or (b) unless the New Testament gives authority for interpreting them in other than a literal sense, or (c) unless a literal interpretation would produce a contradiction with truths, principles, or factual statements contained in non-symbolic books of the New Testament. Another obvious rule to be followed is that the clearest New Testament passages in non-symbolic books are to be the norm for the interpretation of prophecy, rather than obscure or partial revelations contained in the Old Testament. In other words we should accept the clear and plain parts of Scripture as a basis for getting the true meaning of the more difficult parts of Scripture.[3]

We should remember, therefore, that the whole message of the Revelation is couched in figurative language and should be so considered in interpretation. Each symbol represents an idea or a spiritual truth. After we get the picture of the symbol in our minds, then we should always ask this question: "What spiritual truth or principle is John trying to set out by his use of this symbol?" The symbol itself is not the truth, but it is a vehicle used of God to express a certain aspect of truth. In order to arrive at this truth, we must consider the symbol in the light of its context, never apart from it. The symbol can only be understood as it is studied in the light of its use in the context.

At this point it is impossible to consider all of the symbols found in the Apocalypse. Most of them will be studied in greater detail as we come to them in the particular passages. However, a few of them are so prominent throughout the book that we will do well to point out something of their significance in this introductory study. This will also help to set the stage for our understanding of all the symbols.

Numbers played an important role in the symbolism which John used in the Apocalypse. In fact, through the ages the Jews have attached symbolic significance to certain numbers. No one can read the Revelation without being impressed with the frequency of the number seven. It appears fifty-seven times in this book and more than seven hundred times in the whole Bible. To mention only a few: There are seven days in the week; seven days of grace for Noah before entering the ark; seven years of work by Jacob for Rachel; seven bows by Jacob before Esau; seven years of plenty; seven years of famine; seven days of marching around Jericho; seven locks in Samson's hair; seven years in the building of the Temple; seven days of silence before Job; seven days of the Feast of the Tabernacles. On and on we could go, but space forbids it.

In the Revelation we are confronted with seven churches, seven spirits, seven candlesticks, seven stars, seven lamps, seven seals, seven horns, seven eyes, seven angels, seven thunders, seven heads, seven crowns, seven plagues, seven bowls, and seven mountains. No serious student could doubt that there must be some significance to the frequency of this number in the Bible and in the

Apocalypse. Seven has long been recognized by the Jews as a symbol of that which is complete or perfect. When the Jews used the number seven, they usually had more in mind than mere arithmetic. The number seven looms large in the Apocalypse because this is the complete story of redemption. John purposely uses this number frequently in order to impress upon his readers that this is the complete story.

Other numbers are also symbolic in significance. Some of the more commonly used ones are these: two, the number which symbolizes attestation of a fact; three, the divine number depicting the Trinity; four, the earthly number suggested by the four directions of the wind and the four dimensions of earthly things; seven, the sum of three and four, carrying the idea of completion; five, the number which signifies that which is material or finite (five senses, five fingers, five toes, or in its multiples of ten, twenty, one hundred, one thousand, which only serve to intensify the idea); six, the number just short of seven which signifies failure; and twelve (or any of its multiples), the product of three times four, God manifested in his universe. (It speaks of God's divine plan in his created universe, or, as Dr. W. A. Criswell expresses it, "the elective purpose of God in the story of human life.") [4] We will have occasion to observe the use of these numerical symbols as we get into the actual interpretation of the text.

There are many other symbols to be found in the Apocalypse besides the numbers. Perhaps we

should mention just a few of them here in order
to show how they are used.

Take for instance the word Babylon, which is
used six times in the book. In describing the downfall of the wicked citadel, the seat of godless rule,
John uses this term. Babylon was an ancient city
noted for its wickedness and godlessness but had
long since gone into oblivion. Obviously John was
referring to the wicked citadel of Rome, the seat
of the godless government of the blaspheming
Domitian. He dared not use the name of Rome;
doing so would be interpreted by the censors as
a plot to overthrow the government. Since Babylon
was known to most people as a city and center
of wickedness, John used it as a symbol of Rome.
In all likelihood his readers understood what he
meant.

Some of the symbols John was able to identify;
others he could not because of the circumstances.
When using the symbol of the great red dragon,
he could without fear identify him clearly as the
devil. The Roman censors would not object to this.
But when he wished to speak of the Roman Emperor himself, he could only use the symbol of
the beast. This symbol is used twenty-two times
by John. The emperor is never clearly identified
in words, but there are ample implications to assure the readers of his identity. The principle of
wickedness embodied in this godless dictator may
well be applied to any similar totalitarian ruler
of any age, but in John's mind it was Domitian,
the nefarious enemy and persecutor of Christians.

Another frequently used symbol in the book is Lamb, which always has reference to Jesus Christ. This symbol appears twenty-eight times in portraying the Christ. The Roman censor may not have been familiar with this term, but every Christian knows that Jesus is the Lamb of God who takes away the sin of the world. There could have been no mistake here. Thus the central personality throughout the whole of the apocalyptic visions is Jesus Christ. This Lamb of God deserves the central and chief place, for he is worthy.

In the light of the foregoing considerations concerning the historical background and symbolic nature of the book of Revelation, there are five words of advice or caution which need to be brought before the mind of the reader as we approach these expository studies.

The first word of advice is that we keep on the main track. One of the most serious dangers facing the student of the Apocalypse is the danger of allowing himself to become sidetracked on some minor issue. It is easy to become so absorbed in some minor aspect of a symbol or a date that one loses all sense of the main theme. The result is a distorted picture and an erroneous interpretation.

We must remember that John had one thing in mind—to encourage the downtrodden Christians of Asia Minor by revealing to them the inevitable ultimate victory of the redeemed over all of the forces of evil. The book is a picture of God's redemptive program from beginning to end, showing its triumphant consummation. As we proceed in our study, let us never lose sight of this main theme. We must seek to fit the pieces into this master plan. Every verse of it is related to this primary theme. When we lose sight of this theme, we lose ourselves in a maze of confusion, stultification, and sophism.

In the second place, let us be sure that we understand the nature of redemption. We are using the term redemption here in its wider and more general sense—not in the sense of the salvation of the individual soul only, but in the sense of the total program by which God accomplishes ultimate and complete victory for his people and ultimate and complete defeat for the devil and his cohorts. To be sure, God's program of redemption does include the salvation of the individual soul; but it is more than this. God is not through when he saves the individual soul from the consequences of his sin. His program includes a plan by which he provides complete victory for the righteous over the wicked. God's redemptive program includes the redemption of the whole world from the ravages caused by sin and Satan. Here in the Revelation John is thinking of redemption in this larger and more comprehensive sense.

There is very little said in the book about the application of redemption to the individual soul, though it is implied in many places. Here we see the unfolding of God's great and glorious redemption in its every aspect. Often when we think of redemption, we think only of the work of Christ on the cross. This is indeed a vital part of redemption, but not all of it. Redemption, in its fullest sense, takes us back into the councils of eternity. It includes everything that God has done or will do in accomplishing complete redemption for man and his world. It is past, present, and future. Dr. W. A. Criswell is right in saying that "there is a future in that word 'redemption' that encompasses the entire consummation of the purposes and elective decrees of God." [5]

In the third place, let us try to forget the time element. We creatures of this earth are plagued with the tendency to try to fit everything into an exacting time schedule. Especially is this true when we approach the study of the book of Revelation. We insist that everything in it must be timed. We live in a time-conscious age. We live by the second hand on the watch, and the question which looms large in the discussion of any subject is "When?" This proclivity, however, is not exactly new to our generation. Men have always been interested to some degree in the time element. When Jesus talked about his coming kingdom his disciples asked, "When shall these things be?" (Matt. 24:3). And when the resurrected Christ stood before his disciples to charge them with the responsibility of witnessing and to assure them of the infilling of his Holy Spirit, they responded by asking, "Lord, wilt thou at this time restore again the kingdom to Israel?" (Acts 1:6). Thus has it been through the centuries. We are often far more concerned about when an event is to take

place than we are with the true significance of
that event.

Actually we cannot completely ignore the time
element, for we live in a time age; however, we
do stand in danger of missing the primary significance of principles and events by giving too much
attention to the time element. This is the mistake
that many have made in their interpretation of
the Apocalypse.

The complete and glorious program of redemption is unfolded before our eyes in this book. It
is unfolded in seven dramatic scenes or episodes.
It is the drama of redemption. Each episode magni-
fies a certain aspect of redemption. These are not
events which follow one another in chronological
order; they are manifestations of certain features
or factors in the redemptive program of our Lord.
They are given to us in logical order, but not necessarily in chronological order. From the standpoint
of time there is much overlapping.

It is a mistake to make these scenes fit into a
rigid time schedule, assigning, as some have done,
each episode to a certain age or dispensation according to the calendar. There are many different
versions of the attempt to chronicle these revealed
features of the redemptive program. Some take
these same general divisions we have noted and
make each division fit into a certain age or dispensation. Others make a different division but still
insist on a chronological order. For instance, W.
Hendriksen also makes seven divisions (different
from ours) but insists that each division gives a

complete history of redemption from the first coming of Christ to the second coming.[6] B. H. Carroll sees in these visions a history of the Roman Catholic Church, each episode depicting a certain era in the church's history.[7]

Dr. W. A. Criswell divides the book into three main divisions: (1) the things which were (the vision of Christ in 1:12-20); (2) the things which are (the letters to the seven churches, chapters 2—3); and (3) the things hereafter (chapters 4—22).[8] Dr. Criswell goes on to explain that everything in this main body of the book points to the seven-year period of tribulation at the end of the age. In all of these various interpretations (and many more), the time element stands out predominantly. While we cannot completely ignore the time element, it should at least be kept in the background. We know that the pictures of celebration and eternal destiny are still future from the standpoint of time; yet we must remember that the Lord is not giving to us in this Apocalypse a program which can be conformed to any kind of rigid time schedule. After all, God does not count time as we count time. To him a thousand years are as a day and a day as a thousand years (2 Pet. 3:8).

More and more as I study this Apocalypse of John, I am convinced that God is seeking to reveal to us his triumphant redemptive program from the standpoint of the great factors involved in it—facts which make possible and lead to its ultimate and glorious consummation. Let us not miss the main issue by becoming involved in a maze of timetables or time speculations. Let us push the time element into the background and open our hearts to these great underlying principles of our redemption in Christ.

In the fourth place, let us take note of the symmetrical pattern which we find in the book. There is a beautiful and striking symmetry about these apocalyptic visions. It is no accident that there are seven main divisions or episodes in the drama of redemption depicted for us here. We have already noted that seven is the perfect number. It signifies that which is complete. Here we have the perfect and complete picture of redemption in seven scenes. Not only do we have seven episodes, but each episode contains seven subdivisions or scenes, depicting the various aspects of the main theme of that particular episode. There is one exception to this. When we come to the picture of eternal destiny there are only two subscenes, for there are only two possible aspects of destiny—heaven and hell. These subdivisions are not as clearly marked in some of the divisions as they are in others, but a careful study will reveal the seven subdivisions in each episode.

Another interesting feature of the format is the presence of an interlude between the sixth and seventh subdivisions of each main episode. This interlude will vary in length from one verse to a whole chapter. It may contain a doxology of praise or the explanation of some feature of the foregoing scene. In every case the seventh symbol is transitional. It closes out one series of symbols and introduces the next series. This pattern is significantly followed throughout the book, giving to the total picture a balance and symmetry which cannot be overlooked. It leaves one with the impression that this is not something hastily put together in haphazard form or with little continuity. There is a most striking continuity of thought running throughout the book, of which the discerning reader will not be unmindful.

Our fifth and last word of advice is this: Let us never forget the point of view. The fourth chapter begins with a reference to an open door into heaven. "After this I looked, and, behold, a door was opened in heaven: and the first voice which I heard was as it were of a trumpet talking with me; which said, Come up hither, and I will shew thee things which must be hereafter" (v. 1). John is invited to stand in this door opened into heaven to watch the unfolding of this drama of redemption. It is important that we remember John's point of view. This is not to say that what John saw actually took place in heaven. What John saw takes place in heaven and on earth, but John was privileged to see it as it looks from heaven's point of view.

One's point of view does make a difference in what he sees. Especially is this true when one is looking at God's redemptive program. As we see it from earth's point of view, it does not look very good. In fact, it can become very depressing, and this is exactly what had taken place in the hearts of these Christians of Asia Minor. They looked

out from their vantage point to see nothing but
the rise of satanic power and the suppression of
the gospel witness. What they saw was most discouraging, even as it is also discouraging as we
look at it today. We see Christianity apparently
losing ground to the communistic advance. Evil,
it seems, is running rampant everywhere. Genuine
dedicated Christians are becoming more and more
difficult to find. Are we really losing the battle?
It certainly looks like it when we see it from earth's
point of view. If I looked at it very long with realis-
tic eyes, I could become as despondent and discouraged as these Christian of Asia Minor in the
first century.

We are not personally able to look at this unfolding drama from heaven's point of view. However, God has made it possible for us to look
through the eyes of John at this unfolding drama
seen from heaven's point of view. This is the dis-
tinctive feature of the message of the Revelation.
It portrays God's redemptive program from heav-
en's point of view. What a blessed privilege! Let
us try to forget where we are. Closing out the world
around us, let us go with the beloved John up the
elevator until we stand just behind him, looking
through this door opened into heaven. What we
shall see will thrill our souls and lift us out of
any slough of despondency. This is the picture
of redemption as God sees it, and it is a marvelous
thing to behold. It is like looking at a cloud from
the upward side. From the ground the cloud looks
dark and foreboding; but when one takes an air-

plane and rides above the cloud, he sees an entirely different picture. From that vantage point he sees the beautiful reflection of the sun on the fleecy clouds—bright and inspiring sight. In the book of Revelation we are flying above the clouds, looking down on the movements of history as they are seen in God's eyes. All things are seen in a different light and from a different perspective.

When we have finished our flight with John to the heavenly threshold, we shall rejoice with unspeakable joy and will face the realities of this earthly struggle with new courage and determination, for we will then know something of the glorious and triumphant consummation of this redemptive program of which we are a part. We shall be shown things that are yet to be, but in showing us these things "hereafter" we will see the picture in its entirety, beginning with eternity and closing with eternity.

CHAPTER THREE
Introductory Chapters of the Apocalypse (1—3)

As indicated previously, the first three chapters of the Apocalypse are introductory, and it is with these three chapters that we concern ourselves in this particular part of our study. These three chapters divide themselves rather conveniently into three main divisions. After the statement of purpose which is little more than a subtitle (vv. 1-3), there is a greeting or salutation (vv. 4-9). This is followed by a preliminary vision of Christ (vv. 10-20). The last division of the introduction consists of letters to the seven churches of Asia (chaps. 2 and 3).

The greeting or salutation is rather typical of all first-century Christian letters. There is first an identity of the author, who is John. This is followed by an identification of the intended readers, the seven churches of Asia. The greeting which follows is in the name of the Father, the Holy Spirit, and the Son. The Father is identified as the one "which is, and which was, and which is to come," the eternal One. "The seven Spirits which are before his throne" (v. 4) do not refer to seven distinct spirits, but to the one and only Holy Spirit. Here

we find the first symbol in the book. Seven is the
perfect number. It always symbolizes that which
is perfect and complete. This symbolism was
doubtlessly obvious to the original readers, and
it prepared them for the more difficult symbols
to follow. Jesus Christ is clearly identified as the
"faithful witness, and the first begotten of the
dead, and the prince of the kings of the earth"
(v. 5a). A word is added as to what the Christian
has received through Jesus Christ: "Unto him that
loved us, and washed us from our sins in his own
blood, and hath made us kings and priests unto
God and his Father" (vv. 5b-6a). How comforting
this thought must have been to those persecuted
Christians of Asia!

The doxology which follows was often used by
the Christians of the first century: "Unto him be
glory and dominion for ever and ever. Amen" (v.
6b). This is followed by a very brief reference to
the return of Christ to this earth: "Behold, he cometh with clouds; and every eye shall see him, and
they also which pierced him; and all kindreds of
the earth shall wail because of him. Even so,
Amen" (v. 7). After reiterating the thought of the
eternal and sovereign nature of God, John closes
the salutation with a simple statement as to his
present location and the reason for it. He is a
fellow-sufferer and has been exiled to the Isle of
Patmos "for the word of God, and for the testimony
of Jesus Christ" (v. 9).

The rest of the first chapter is given to a description of a vision of Christ, which John was privi-

leged to see while on the Isle of Patmos. This is
a preliminary vision and sets the stage and tone
for the rest of the Apocalypse. There seems to
be a dual purpose in the injection of this preliminary vision. First, it was used to set the stage for
the symbolic nature of the message which he is
about to deliver to these Christians of Asia Minor.
This vision is obviously symbolic in every respect.
Some of these symbols John is able to identify.
He tells his readers very plainly that the seven
golden lampstands represent the seven churches
of Asia. He also explains that the seven stars represent the seven angels of these churches. Most
of the expositors think that John was speaking
here of the pastors of these churches. The word
is usually translated angel; however, etymologi-
cally the word means messenger. The idea of messenger or pastor seems to be more appropriate
in the light of the context.

These two symbols are clearly identified simply
because they could be identified without arousing
the suspicion of the Roman censors. At the same
time John could give his readers a clue as to the
nature of the message he was about to give to
them. By thus identifying these two symbols John
was saying in effect: "I am about to talk to you
in the form of figures and symbols. Please be on
the lookout for these symbols and watch closely
for the clues as to their significance."

There is another apparent reason for this preliminary vision of Christ. It helped these discouraged
Christians of Asia to get a proper perspective of

Christ. So much had gone against them because they were Christians that they had begun to wonder if Christ had forsaken them or had been dethroned. This vision gave them fresh assurance concerning their Lord.

The fact that this is a vision of Christ cannot be questioned, even though the name of Christ is nowhere mentioned in it. John describes the figure which he saw as one "like unto the Son of man" (v. 13). Actually, the article does not appear in the original language, and the later translations give it more correctly as "a son of man." The absence of any reference to Jesus Christ by name is understandable. Just before giving the vision, John does refer to the historic fact that he is on the Isle of Patmos "for the word of God, and for the testimony of Jesus Christ" (v. 9). This he could do without any difficulty because he was simply stating a fact, the reason for his exile. But when he proceeded to depict this Christ in all of his sovereign and majestic state, he dared not identify him by name. In such a case the Roman censor would have sensed that John was promoting a rival to the emperor of Rome.

There is no doubt but that the readers understood the veiled identity. They remembered quite well that Jesus referred to himself more than eighty times in the Gospels as "the Son of man."

When we put the pieces of this picture together, we are able to see a man whose hair is long and white, wearing a robe flowing down to his feet. A golden girdle was worn at his breast. His feet shone with the glitter of brass being burned in a hot furnace. His eyes were like glowing balls of fire. Out of his mouth proceeded a long and sharp two-edged sword. He was uttering something which sounded like the roar of a mighty waterfall. His whole face shone forth with a radiance like the glow of a noonday sun.

Let us remember that this is not a literal picture of the Christ. Some of the symbols are somewhat unusual and even grotesque. If you should meet such a person as you were coming home on a dark night, you would be frightened. It is no wonder that John fell as dead at the feet of such a character. I am sure that I, too, would have passed out from sheer fright at such a sight. Try to put this picture together and then draw a mental image of it! Surely this is not a true and literal picture of the Christ! Surely this is not what we shall expect to see when we stand before him in his glory!

Yes, this is a true picture of the Christ, but it is not a literal one. John is able to give accent to certain features of the Christ by the use of such weird imagery. The Eastern mind was oriented to such imagery better than the twentieth-century American mind. But we too can grasp the lessons if we understand the nature of the symbolism. We do not mean to say by this that John himself concocted these figures in his own mind. He actually saw what he described. God gave him the vision and John merely recorded what he saw.

God was trying to say something to these Christians of Asia and to us through this beloved apostle. As we ponder this strange image of the Christ which has been painted before us, at least three lessons stand out—three features of the Christ of which every Christian should be aware at all times, especially in times of distress and persecution.

The first thing God seems to be saying to us through this vision is that Christ is alive. There he stands with all of the characteristics of life. As John falls at his feet, we see this majestic figure as he reaches down to touch John. Then we listen as he speaks: "Fear not; I am the first, and the last: I am he that liveth, and was dead; and, behold, I am alive for evermore. Amen" (vv. 17-18).

More precious than the fact that Christ is alive is the fact that he is triumphantly alive. It is one thing to exist, but it is another thing to exist in triumph. God wanted his dear children in Asia to know more than the mere fact that Jesus was still in existence. He wanted them to know that he was living in sovereignty. The vision, from beginning to end, is one of triumph and majesty. The long flowing robe speaks of royalty and dignity. The jetting balls of fire speak of his penetrating gaze. The sharp two-edged sword speaks of power for cutting down every enemy. The mighty roaring voice as of many waters speaks of authority. When you add to this the statement that Christ himself made, "I have the keys of hell and of death" (v. 18), you have a picture of power and triumph.

There is a third blessed aspect of the Christ

which we are able to see through this vision. This triumphantly alive Christ is not far from us. He is always near. John depicts this Christ as one who is walking in the midst of the seven golden candlesticks. The candlesticks, John explains, are the seven churches. This means that Christ is walking in the midst of his churches. He is not far removed in some remote spot, looking on from afar; rather, he walks by our side. Not only does he walk in the midst of the churches, but he also holds the messengers of these churches in his right hand.

With this vision of Christ before our eyes, we turn to the letters to the seven churches. One glance at these letters and we are immediately arrested by two things. The first is the presence of that number seven. There are seven churches: Ephesus, Smyrna, Pergamos, Thyatira, Sardis, Philadelphia, and Laodicea. Why are only seven churches mentioned? And why these particular seven? These were by no means all of the churches in existence in Asia Minor at the time John wrote. We are quite sure that there was a church at Colossae, and there were certainly others. We cannot say why these particular seven were chosen, unless these seven formed somewhat of a circle geographically. A glance at the map will show this to be true.

But there was more to it than geography. The number seven always signified to the Jews and early Christians the idea of completion or perfection. The number seven was obviously used here because it was symbolic of the total Christian community. According to this symbolism, these letters are addressed to all churches of all times and all places. They are representative of all the churches. Every church in existence is a prototype of one of these seven churches, or it may be a combination of two or three of them. The fact is that every church fits into this pattern somewhere and is, therefore, a proper subject for these addresses. Churches may have changed in some respects since the days of the New Testament, but their problems are still essentially the same as those faced by these churches of the first century.

The second thing which arrests our attention is the reference to the churches rather than to the church: "the churches which are in Asia" (vv. 4,11). This leads me to believe that as late as the closing decade of the first century, there was still no conception of the church in a hierarchical sense. The emphasis throughout the New Testament is upon the local congregation. The sense of a church as an ecclesiastical hierarchy composed of all the local congregations is a much later development.

In looking at the letters themselves, we are impressed with five characteristics which are common to all seven of them. In the first place, it should be noted that each letter begins with an identity of the church addressed; and in each case the letter is addressed to "the angel" of that church. As noted above, by "angel" he was perhaps referring to the pastor of the church. This is followed immediately with an identity of the author, who is Christ. John is simply the instrument through whom Christ speaks.

It is interesting to note that Christ identifies himself in each letter by using some part of the preliminary vision which appears in the first chapter. In each case he refers to an aspect of the character of Christ which is especially appropriate for the circumstances existing in that particular church. The name "Jesus Christ" is not once mentioned in these letters, but from the symbolic identity given at the beginning of each letter there could have been no doubt in the minds of the readers as to the author of the letter.

To the church at Ephesus he is the one "that holdeth the seven stars in his right hand, who walketh in the midst of the seven golden candlesticks" (2:1).

To the church at Smyrna, he is "the first and the last, which was dead, and is alive" (2:8).

To the church at Pergamos, he is the one "which hath the sharp sword with two edges" (2:12).

To the church at Thyatira, he is "the Son of God, who hath his eyes like unto a flame of fire, and his feet are like fine brass" (2:18).

To the church at Sardis, he is the one "that hath the seven Spirits of God, and the seven stars" (3:1).

To the church at Philadelphia, he is the one "that is holy, he that is true, he that hath the key of David, he that openeth, and no man shutteth; and shutteth, and no man openeth" (3:7).

To the church at Laodicea, he is "the Amen,

the faithful and true witness, the beginning of the creation of God" (3:14).

When we put all of these together, we have the same picture of Christ which is given in the last part of the first chapter.

In the second place, each letter contains a statement concerning the familiarity of Christ with that particular situation. He wants them to know that he is not speaking as one who calls from a distance, but as one who is near enough to understand their weaknesses, their virtues, and their needs. The consciousness of our Lord's familiarity with our needs is always very comforting and encouraging.

In the third place, each letter contains a message for that particular church. The content is not the same in any two letters; however, generally speaking, two things are common to all the letters with one exception in each area. In all but one, the content of the letter begins with a word of commendation, the exception being the letter to the Laodiceans; and in all but one this is followed by a word of rebuke or reprimand, the exception being in the letter to Smyrna. The content of the letter in each case gives some insight into the predominant characteristics of that particular church. We have space for only a brief summary of the outstanding characteristics of each church. They are as follows.

The church at Ephesus had a good defense but a weak offense. The Christians at Ephesus were sound in doctrine and courageous in defending sound doctrine. Jesus said to them, "I know thy works, and thy labour, and thy patience, and how thou canst not bear them which are evil; and thou hast tried them which say they are apostles, and are not, and hast found them liars" (2:2). This speaks of doctrinal soundness. But then he goes on to say, "Nevertheless I have somewhat against thee, because thou hast left thy first love" (2:4). In other words, they had lost the fervor of that love which they had for Christ when first they believed. This is to say that they had lost their evangelistic zeal.

The church at Smyrna was the suffering church. All of these Christians of Asia had suffered untold agonies at the hands of Domitian, the wicked Roman emperor; but it seems that Smyrna had been given a double portion of this suffering. The admonition which Jesus gave to Smyrna speaks of this: "Fear none of those things which thou shalt suffer: behold, the devil shall cast some of you into prison, that ye may be tried; and ye shall have tribulation ten days; be thou faithful unto death, and I will give thee a crown of life" (2:10). But even with all of their poverty and woe, they were wealthy in spiritual blessings. They were poor in this world's goods, but rich in faith.

The church at Pergamos was a counterpart to the church at Ephesus. Here was a church which seemed to have some measure of evangelistic zeal, even to the point of martyrdom; but it was somewhat lacking in doctrinal soundness. Jesus rebuked them for allowing false doctrines to go unchallenged in their midst.

The church at Thyatira appears before us as a growing church. Having enumerated some of their good works, such as love, service, faith, and patience, Jesus noted that their latter works were more than their earlier works. This is growth. They did have some problems with a certain "Jezebel" (2:20); but in spite of this, they were growing. A growing church always has problems. The only church that doesn't have problems is a dead one.

The Sardis church is easily identified as the dead church. They had all the forms of life without the essence of it. Theirs was an empty shell; however, even in this pathetic situation there was at least one bright spot. There were some who had not defiled their garments. Hence, there was some hope even for Sardis.

The Philadelphia church was the missionary church. Jesus indicated in his letter that he had opened a door before them and they had proceeded to enter. This is a happy situation. Taking advantage of opportunities for evangelism and service often entails sacrifice and suffering, but blessed is that church which is disposed to do it.

The Laodicean church is perhaps the most deplorable of the seven. It was the self-satisfied church. The members were resting on their laurels, thinking that they had it made. They felt no sense of need. They proudly boasted of their many assets. They were neither cold nor hot, just complacent. Therefore, Jesus threatens to "spue" them out of his mouth—that is, to vomit them up (3:16).

In the fourth place, each letter contains a beautiful promise. A study of these promises will be most rewarding; however, a detailed study of these is not permissible within the time and space limits allotted for this study. Suffice it to say here that every situation includes a precious promise. The situation may be ever so dark and dismal, but God provides a promise of hope. Even for the church at Laodicea, Jesus held out a promise which may well have been intended for all of the churches: "Behold, I stand at the door, and knock: if any man hear my voice, and open the door, I will come in to him, and will sup with him, and he with me" (3:20). Let us never forget that God has a precious promise to fit every situation. Let us learn to rest upon these promises and look beyond the darkness into the light of them.

In the fifth place, let us take note of the fact that each letter closes with an exhortation to hear and heed. Toward the close of each letter there is a repetition of this simple but significant phrase: "He that hath an ear, let him hear what the Spirit saith unto the churches" (2:7,11,13,29; 3:6,13,22). Such a word of exhortation may seem trite; yet it is needful. We cannot be reminded too often of the importance of listening to the voice of the Spirit which speaks to us through the written and spoken Word. It is the same as saying, "Now listen; keep your ears open." He who does not keep an open ear turned toward the Spirit of God will miss the blessing. Especially is this true as we approach the study of this last book in our Bible. A casual or cursory reading will not suffice to get the message. Undivided attention must be given. We must bend our ears with earnest desire if we would grasp the wonderful truths which have been hidden here beneath the symbols but open and available to those who listen for the Spirit's leading in all sincerity. "He that hath an ear, let him hear what the Spirit saith unto the churches." In other words, "Are you listening? Do you have your heart and your ears open? If you do, you are in for a rich experience."

CHAPTER FOUR

The Sovereign God
(4—5)

The first vision or episode in the unfolding drama of redemption reveals a majestic and sovereign God. This is the first and basic factor in the story of redemption.

As the curtain rises on this first scene, John sees a throne and someone sitting on it. This one who sits upon the throne is not identified until we come to the eighth verse of the fourth chapter, but it is obvious from the beginning that he is God himself. This opening scene must have given much comfort to the oppressed Christians of Asia Minor, for in the midst of so much sin, greed, and persecution they had begun to wonder if God had not been dethroned by these mighty forces of Satan which seemed to run roughshod over everything and everybody.

Here we have the proper beginning for any understanding of redemption or of world history. We must begin with God on his throne. This is the one and only proper starting point in any discussion of man, his world, and his destiny. Any other starting point can only bring the mind into a state of confusion. But this is the mistake which many have made and are making in our modern scientific world. We have tried to understand the deeper things of life by beginning with some scientific fact which we already have in hand. We think that we can understand the supernatural by beginning with the natural and reasoning back to the supernatural. But this process never yields a satisfactory answer. It is true that some things can be learned by reasoning from the natural to the supernatural, but by such a system of reasoning we can never arrive at an adequate answer to the great perplexing problems of life.

This is the weakness of much of our modern-day philosophy, even some of our religious philosophy. For instance, the system of religious philosophy known as existentialism is based upon this kind of reasoning. It begins with man's own mind or man's own experience and seeks to reason from that up to God. It immediately eliminates all that cannot be conformed to the individual's own mind or intelligence. The result is a state of confusion and bewilderment. Such philosophies have contributed little, if anything, to man's understanding of God and his universe. They are continually reaching out for something which they never are able to grasp. They talk about the meaning of existence in high-sounding but nebulous terms which nobody really seems to understand, not even those who write about it. Those who are caught up by the spirit of intellectualism which it generates are not only robbed of the anchor which a simple faith gives, but they are also given nothing but uncertainties to take its place.

In any system of reasoning, be it ever so scientific, one must begin with an assumption which he cannot scientifically prove. He can go back only so far; then he must assume something which has no real proof. For many this assumption is the infallibility and sovereignty of the human mind. For instance, if one is discussing the theory of evolution, he may trace his theory back scientifically to a certain point; but somewhere he must assume something which he cannot prove. If he could prove, and this is extremely doubtful, that all life began from the amoeba, then he must assume something as to the cause of the existence of this amoeba. In any line of reasoning on any subject, if one traces it back far enough, he must make an assumption which he cannot prove scientifically.

If, then, in any course of reasoning, one must begin with an assumption, why not begin with the assumption that a sovereign God exists who is the cause of all things and who has a sovereign purpose in all things? I cannot prove this assumption scientifically. I accept it by faith through revelation. To me it is a far more intelligent assumption than the assumption that my own mind is capable of and infallible in understanding the vast intricacies and mysteries of life in all of its varied aspects. This is not to say that I shall not use all of the mentality with which I am equipped in an effort to understand. It only means that I shall begin this effort upon the assumption that there is a sovereign God who sits upon his throne and who works his sovereign will and purpose upon this whole universe.

With this as our starting point, we are in a much better position to understand the meaning of life and destiny. Without it the picture becomes a mass of confusion. A rather standard illustration is the little boy who was told to put the pieces of a picture of the world together, even though he knew absolutely nothing about world geography. Within a very short time he had the picture complete with every piece in its proper place. The father was astonished and asked his son how he could achieve this feat which was apparently impossible. The son explained that he merely turned the pieces over and discovered that they were pieces of the face of Christ. He was familiar with the face of Christ, and soon the task was finished. When he turned the picture back over, there was the picture of the world with each piece in its proper place. When he began with Christ, the whole world fell into its proper place. Whether or not this ever actually happened, we cannot say; but it does illustrate our point. When we begin with God on his throne in sovereignty, the pieces of our jigsaw puzzle concerning man and his world begin to fall into their proper places.

As we look at this unfolding of redemption through the eyes of John, we begin with a sovereign God on his majestic throne. Let us never lose sight of this throne. It must remain the focal point in all of our thinking. Then we will come back to it when we reach the consummation of the story.

Having introduced us to the one who sits upon the throne, John proceeds to show us seven symbols, each of which gives emphasis to some aspect of God's sovereignty and majesty. The picture, as John sees it, is as follows:

"And, behold, a throne was set in heaven, and one sat on the throne. / And he that sat was to look upon like a jasper and a sardine stone; and there was a rainbow round about the throne, in sight like unto an emerald. / And round about the throne were four and twenty seats; and upon the seats I saw four and twenty elders sitting, clothed in white raiment; and they had on their heads crowns of gold. / And out of the throne proceeded lightnings and thunderings and voices; and there were seven lamps of fire burning before the throne, which are the seven Spirits of God. / And before the throne there was a sea of glass like unto crystal; and in the midst of the throne, and round about the throne, were four beasts full of eyes before and behind. / And the first beast was like a lion, and the second beast like a calf, and the third beast had a face as a man, and the fourth beast was like a flying eagle. / And the four beasts had each of them six wings about him; and they were full of eyes within; and they rest not day and night, saying, Holy, holy, holy, Lord God Almighty, which was, and is, and is to come" (4:2-8).

The one who sits upon the throne is himself like a jasper or sardine stone, but there are also seven symbols round and about this throne which point to the majesty and sovereignty of this one who thus sits upon the throne. The first symbol is in the form of an emerald rainbow which encircles the throne. The rainbow has long been recognized as a symbol of God's unfailing promises, ever since that day when it first appeared as Noah and his family disembarked from the ark after the Flood. This rainbow round about the throne served to remind the reader that God had not forgotten his promises to his redeemed people. He is a God of unfailing promise.

The second symbol is in the form of twenty-four elders who sit upon little thrones round about the great throne. At this point we run into some difficulties as we seek to decipher the symbolism. Who are these twenty-four elders and what do they represent? Commentators have differed rather widely on the significance of these elders. We are quite sure that they were symbolic and representative rather than literal, but the true nature of their symbolic significance is not absolutely clear. Some think that these represent the twelve tribes of the Old Testament and the twelve apostles of the New, thus combining the two covenants to include the redeemed of both. Others feel that these twenty-four elders represent the leaders or pastors of the churches, some of whom had already been martyred. The number, twenty-four, is a multiple of twelve, the product of three times four, a symbol of God's manifestation in his universe through divinely ordained institutions. This seems to me to be more feasible, and yet the others are certainly possible. In any case the basic idea seems to be that of a representation of leadership in the kingdom of God. The important thing here, as I see it, is not the identification of the elders but the recognition of what they were doing. They were falling down before the one who sat upon the throne and worshiping him, a symbolic picture which points to the majesty and sovereignty of God.

The third symbol is in the form of lightnings and thunders. These are obviously symbols of God's authority and power. The lightning penetrates, and the thunder speaks of authority. Who is not reminded of the awesome power of God when he sees a sudden burst of light across the sky and then listens to the booming voice of the thunder which follows? So it is in the vision which John saw. It gave accent to the awesome authority of the one who sat upon the throne.

The fourth symbol was in the form of seven lamps burning before the throne. John identifies the seven lamps for us. They are the seven Spirits of God. This is the second time that we have run across this symbolism in the book of Revelation. In his introductory greeting John mentions "the seven Spirits which are before his throne" (1:4). In that instance, however, they are not described as seven lamps burning; but in both instances there are seven Spirits, the number seven being used qualitatively rather than quantitatively. Seven speaks of that which is perfect or complete.

The Holy Spirit is thus depicted as being radiantly present in this heavenly scene, giving light and glory to the one who sits upon the throne. This symbolism is in keeping with the revealed nature of the Holy Spirit. Though he is the third person of the Trinity and as much divine as the other two persons of the Trinity, his avowed purpose is not to glorify himself but to glorify the Son and the Father. Thus the lamp sheds light upon the glory and majesty of the one who sits upon the throne.

The fifth symbol was in the form of a sea of pure water which lay in front of the throne. It was as clear as crystal glass. In ancient times the sea was recognized as a protective barrier. Man had not yet conquered the seas as he has today, and much less the air; therefore, the sea for them was a symbol of security. The idea of the sea in the vision seems to be that of showing the security of God's throne from any encroachment of a hostile power.

The sixth symbol is the most enigmatic of them all. It is in the form of four living creatures. The authorized version has "beasts," but a better translation of the Greek word, *zoa*, is "living creatures," as is found in most of the later versions. Later on in the Apocalypse we will come across the word beast, which is a translation of an altogether different word in the Greek.

There were four of these living creatures. One was like a lion; the second was like a young bullock; the third had the face of a man; and the fourth was like a flying eagle. They had eyes before, behind, and within, and six wings each.

Again we have differences of opinion among the scholars as to the identity of the four living ones. What do they really represent or symbolize? This is not easy to determine. Some hold that these four represent the four basic attributes of deity: strength, patience, intelligence, and swiftness. This interpretation seems to be a little awkward since the four living creatures also worship the one who sits on the throne. Others feel that these four living creatures represent the four general areas of life upon the earth: the lion representing the wild beasts; the young bull, domesticated animals; the flying eagle, the birds; and man. I prefer to think of these four living creatures as representatives of the messengers which are at God's disposal for the executing of his every desire, all of which is another way of saying that this one who sits upon the throne is sovereign in every way. As in the case of the twenty-four elders, the identity of the four living creatures is rather inconsequential. The important thing is to notice what they are doing. They are ascribing praise and honor to him who sits upon the throne.

Having now introduced six of the seven symbols pointing to the sovereignty of the one who sits upon the throne, there follows a brief interlude before the seventh symbol is introduced. This pattern will be followed throughout the seven visions. This interlude is the shortest of them all, but nonetheless significant. It is in the form of a doxology coming from the four and twenty elders and the four living creatures. All of them fall down before the throne and join in a doxology of praise to the one who sits upon the throne. John describes it like this: "And when those beasts give glory and honour and thanks to him that sat on the throne, who liveth for ever and ever, / The four and twenty elders fall down before him that sat on the throne, and worship him that liveth for ever and ever, and cast their crowns before the throne saying, / Thou art worthy, O Lord, to receive glory and honour and power; for thou hast created all things, and for thy pleasure they are and were created" (4:9-11).

The seventh symbol in each series is transitional. It closes one series and introduces the next series. This seventh symbol is a book which lies in the hand of him who sits upon the throne. It was not a bound book as we think of it in this modern era, but a scroll made of papyrus and rolled up and sealed with seven seals. It was written on both sides. We might be in doubt as to the significance of this scroll except for the fact that when, in the next series of symbols, the seven seals are loosed, we can see the awful judgments of God expressed. It is evident, therefore, that this sealed book represents the mighty judgments of a sovereign and righteous God. A sovereign God must be a God of righteous judgment. Thus we have another symbol of God's sovereignty; yet at the same time we are introduced to the next step in the unfolding drama of redemption. These judg-

ments are so full that they must be written on
both sides of the scroll, and there are seven sections of these judgments, with each section being
sealed with a separate seal.

As John looks upon these sealed judgments in
the hand of him who sits upon the throne, an angel
cried out with a loud voice, saying, "Who is worthy to open the book and to loose the seals
thereof?" (5:2). But there was no one to be found
who could open these seals, whereupon John began to cry. Here was the sovereign God with all
of the judgments necessary to effect justice against
the workers of iniquity; yet there was no one to
be found who could open them up and turn them
loose. This disturbed John, but presently one of
the elders spoke to him, saying, "Weep not: behold, the Lion of the tribe of Juda, the Root of
David, hath prevailed to open the book, and to
loose the seven seals thereof" (5:5).

Presently there stood in the midst of the throne
"a Lamb as it had been slain, having seven horns
and seven eyes, which are the seven Spirits of
God sent forth into all the earth" (5:6). This must
have been somewhat surprising to John. He had
been told that the "Lion of the tribe of Juda" had
been found worthy to open the seals; but when
John looked up he saw a lamb, not a lion. Here
we have two aspects of the nature of Christ revealed. As the executor of the righteous judgments
of a sovereign God, Christ is like a lion devouring
its prey; but before he can be qualified to execute
these judgments, he must become a lamb to be

sacrificed as an atonement.

This lamb appeared as one that had been slain, an obvious allusion to the death of Christ on Calvary as the Lamb of God. The seven horns speak of completeness, and the seven eyes point to the Holy Spirit whom he sent forth into the world at his departure from the world. That this symbol points to Jesus Christ no honest student could deny. Already we have been introduced to the Father and the Holy Spirit. Now the Son takes his place alongside of him who sits upon the throne in order to execute his righteous judgments.

As the Lamb reached forth to take the book from the hand of him who sat upon the throne, the hosts of heaven broke forth into a doxology of praise both for the Lamb and for the one who sat upon the throne. Thus is the sovereignty and majesty of the throne shared with the Lamb and with the seven Spirits. The picture is a scintillating one. Let us look at it as John sees and relates it: "And when he had taken the book, the four beasts and four and twenty elders fell down before the Lamb, having every one of them harps and golden vials full of odours, which are the prayers of saints. / And they sung a new song, saying, Thou art worthy to take the book, and to open the seals thereof; for thou wast slain, and hast redeemed us to God by thy blood out of every kindred, and tongue, and people, and nation; / And hast made us unto our God kings and priests; and we shall reign on the earth. / And I beheld, and I heard the voice of many angels round about the throne

and the beasts and the elders; and the number
of them was ten thousand times ten thousand, and
thousands of thousands; / Saying with a loud
voice, Worthy is the Lamb that was slain to receive power, and riches, and wisdom, and
strength, and honour, and glory, and blessing. /
And every creature which is in heaven, and on
the earth, and under the earth, and such as are
in the sea, and all that are in them, heard I saying,
Blessing, and honour, and glory, and power, be
unto him that sitteth upon the throne, and unto
the Lamb for ever and ever. / And the four beasts
said, Amen, and the four and twenty elders fell
down and worshipped him that liveth for ever and
ever" (5:8-14).

Thus is the stage set for the second great episode
in the drama of redemption—a picture of a sovereign and righteous God in judgment. But never
let us lose sight of this beginning and basic scene.
God is on his throne in majestic sovereignty; and
by his side is the Christ, worthy in every respect
because of his atoning sacrifice to execute the
righteous judgments of him who sits upon the
throne. Behind every experience in history stands
this sovereign God. We cannot always understand
his ways and his purposes; but when we recognize,
in the very beginning, his place of sovereignty with
reference to man, the universe, and history, our
understanding will be much more complete and
satisfying. Our first responsibility is that of surren-
dering ourselves to this sovereign God and his
Christ in total commitment of life.

CHAPTER FIVE

The Righteous Judgments
(6:1 to 8:5)

As the first act closed in the unfolding drama of redemption, we saw in the hand of him who sat upon the throne a scroll rolled up and sealed with seven seals. A Lamb appears who is the only one worthy and able to open the seals. Written upon this scroll are the righteous judgments of a righteous God. In this first scene we are not told what is written upon this scroll, but the loosing of the seals by the Lamb in the second series of symbols makes it quite clear that this scroll contains the judgments of a righteous God. They are executed by the Lamb.

He is not only a God of sovereignty and majesty but also a God of righteousness. In righteousness he must express judgment upon those who defy him and transgress his holy law. If he did not do this, he would be neither sovereign nor righteous. In his sovereignty he rules in righteousness. This means that he must deal in judgment with those who refuse to submit to his sovereignty. Therefore, in logical order, the second series of symbols introduces us to our sovereign God of righteousness. As each seal is broken, some aspect of God's righ-

teous judgment is depicted. These are not succes-
sive acts of history in some kind of chronological
order; rather, they are symbols which represent
the instruments of judgment which are available
to our righteous God. To John and his readers they
may have pointed to some current event or incident in Roman history, but in our interpretation
of the message we must see here the instruments
of judgment which are available to our righteous
God. God has used them, is using them, and will
use them in bringing judgment and retribution
upon the enemies of God and of God's redeemed
people.

The present manifestations of God's judgments
are depicted in the apocalyptic vision in the form
of four horsemen. The variety of interpretation
about these four horsemen of the Apocalypse cov-
ers a very wide range. Here as in some other
places in interpretation, we cannot afford to be
too dogmatic. There is certainly room here for a
variety of interpretation, but some of the interpretations are so fantastic and irrelevant that they
do not make good sense. Any interpretation which
does not take into account the obvious tone of
judgment which runs all through this series of symbols makes little sense. We may not be able in
every instance to pinpoint the particular aspect
of God's judgment, but the fact that each symbol
does point to some aspect of judgment cannot be
denied. With this understanding of the overall tone
of the whole series, we shall attempt to interpret
the meaning and significance of each of the seven

symbols in the series under discussion.

The first four seem to refer to the present instruments of God's judgment upon a godless people. As the Lamb looses the first seal, one of the four living creatures cries out, "Come and see" (v. 1). John sees a white horse coming forth, on which is a rider wearing a crown and carrying a bow in his hand. He goes forth "conquering, and to conquer" (v. 2). Some think that this white horse and its rider represent Christ himself, but this would make the situation somewhat awkward since Christ is the one who opens the seal, bringing forth the rider on the white horse. Others, like Lenski,[1] think that this rider on the white horse represents the Word of God, which goes forth conquering and to conquer. It is difficult to see how either of these fits into the pattern of judgment.

More in keeping with the theme of judgment is the position of men like W. A. Criswell [2] and J. B. Lawrence,[3] who look upon this symbol as representing the Antichrist; however, there is a difference of opinion even with these. Dr. Lawrence thinks of this Antichrist in relation to past, present, and future history, while Dr. Criswell would limit his operation to that seven-year period at the end of the age known as the period of tribulation. In both of these interpretations the appearance of the Antichrist becomes the occasion for the trials and the tribulations which are represented in the three horsemen which follow.

Such an interpretation does have a relationship to the idea of judgment, but it does not seem to be the most feasible of the possible interpretations. It seems to me more feasible to think that the symbolism here represents invasion or conquest. This is the simplest and most obvious interpretation in the light of the whole picture. This view is also held by such scholars as H. E. Dana,[4] Ray Summers,[5] and A. H. Baldinger.[6] What John seems to be saying is that God's judgment is expressed by the invasion of one nation upon another. The interesting thing is that God often works his judgments through man—that is, using one man or group of men to administer judgment upon another man or group of men, or one nation upon another nation, even when the first is unaware of it.

Let us not forget that we are thinking here of redemption in its wider sense of all that God does to bring complete and final victory to the righteous children of God against the forces of evil. One instrument he uses to accomplish this objective is invasion or conquest. The principle may be applied in any era; but for John and his readers, it pointed to the Parthians who dwelt just to the east of the Roman Empire and from time to time dealt severe injury to the Roman nation by invasions into the Empire from the east. It is a well-known fact of history that these Parthian soldiers rode on white horses and used bows and arrows. Though they never conquered Rome, they did inflict serious damage on the eastern section of the empire and kept the wicked empire from achieving some of its objectives. They came out to conquer and did conquer to some extent. Though the Christians of Asia Minor may have thought of the Parthians, the principle thus expressed is a timeless one.

Through the ages God has brought judgment upon wicked nations through invasions by other nations, even other wicked nations. When God wanted to bring judgment upon his own people Israel, he raised up the Assyrians and the Babylonians to administer that judgment. The prophet Habakkuk was quite disturbed at the thought of God's allowing a wicked and blasphemous nation such as Babylon to run roughshod over God's own chosen people. Even though Judah had disobeyed God she was not an avowed godless nation such as Babylon. But God assured the prophet that when he was through using the Babylonians to administer chastisement upon his people, he would see to it that Babylon would receive its just judgment.

When the second seal was lifted, out came a red horse whose rider was given power to take peace from the earth. This naturally follows invasion. The rider on this red horse carried in his hand a great sword. Most scholars agree that this horse symbolizes war in general with its bloodshed. It also includes personal strife, which frequently leads to bloodshed. The cause of war, in nearly every case, is the invasion of a foreign power. A nation may start a war by invading something which is precious to another nation, or a nation may go to war because it feels that it has been invaded. Thus through efforts at conquest, war is generated with all of its bloodshed and destruction. God uses war as a means of judgment.

When the third seal was loosed, out came a black horse, whose rider carried a pair of scales in his hands. A voice was then heard, saying, "A measure of wheat for a penny, and three measures of barley for a penny; and see thou hurt not the oil and the wine" (v. 6). This is evidently a picture of famine, another instrument of judgment in the hands of a righteous God. The basic foods such as wheat and barley are rationed at a premium price. The word here for penny is *denarius*, which would correspond to about fifty cents in American money. In the days in which John lived this represented a full day's pay. In other words, it would take a full day's pay to buy enough wheat for one day's supply, not to speak of the other expenses necessary for living or the other people living in the household. The oil and the wine, which were luxuries, were available in good measure; but the basic foods were scarce and at a premium. They had to be rationed out. The picture is quite clear: It is one of famine with all of its ravages. This is another instrument by which God administers righteous judgment.

The fourth horse was a pale green. The word which John uses here is the word from which we get our English word *chlorine*, a pale green substance. The name of the rider is indicated as death. He was given power over a fourth of the earth "to kill with sword, and with hunger, and with death, and with the beasts of the earth" (v. 8). This picture is one of pestilence, epidemic, and destruction in general.

With such instruments as these God moves through history to administer judgment upon godless people and godless nations. Such movements of God were in evidence during the days of John, but they have been in operation in every generation and will continue to be until the consummation of the age. The picture is a timeless one.

The opening of the fifth seal introduces us, not to another instrument of judgment, but to an explanation for the occasion of these judgments. The picture is still one of judgment, but we are looking at it from a different point of view. At the opening of this fifth seal John saw under the altar the souls of them that had been martyred because of their allegiance to Christ. As John looked he heard them crying out with words such as these: "How long, O Lord, holy and true, doest thou not judge and avenge our blood on them that dwell on the earth?" (v. 10). These were given white robes and told to "rest yet for a little season, until their fellow-servants also and their brethren, that should be killed as they were, should be fulfilled" (v. 11).

It is difficult to reconcile this statement with the idea that all of these visions have to do with the judgment of God during the period of the great tribulation at the end of the age, after the Christians have been raptured out of the world. Here these martyred saints are told very specifically

that there are other Christians ("their brethren")
still living on the earth who are yet to be martyred
as they were.

The dispensationalist makes an attempt to explain this "apparent" difficulty by saying that the
"brethren" referred to in this text are those who
have been converted during the tribulation period.
But if one assumes the pretribulation theory of
the coming of Christ and the rapture of the church
before the seven-year tribulation period, an inex-
plicable contradiction arises. If Jesus comes to rapture the saints and to take the Holy Spirit out of
the world, how can souls be converted who are
left behind? Such a situation is untenable.

Here again we see the foolishness of trying to
fit the apocalyptic visions into an exacting eschatological timetable. In fact, it is not necessary to
try to pinpoint this picture from the standpoint
of time. John is simply showing through this symbolic picture the reason for God's judgments upon
the world. It is in response to the oppressions and
persecutions inflicted upon God's redeemed people. He is a God of retribution, and he will in
due time administer full retribution in return for
the damage done by the devil and his cohorts on
earth.

We sometimes, like these martyred saints, become a little impatient; but let us remember that
this is not our responsibility. It is ours to preach
the Word even to the point of dying in the doing
of it if necessary. God will take care of the retribution in due time. He is not unmindful of the oppres-

sions and cries of his persecuted people. God's redemptive program includes not only the saving of the individual soul, but the full measure of retribution against those who defy and despise God and his redeemed people.

Lest these martyred saints or the oppressed living saints in Asia Minor become overly impatient, God gives to them a brief but startling preview of the final judgment. This preview appears when the Lamb has opened the sixth seal. It is an awesome and fearful sight which meets John's eyes as this sixth seal is lifted from its place. "Lo, there was a great earthquake; and the sun became black as sackcloth of hair, and the moon became as blood; / And the stars of heaven fell unto the earth, even as a fig tree casteth her untimely figs, when she is shaken of a mighty wind. / And the heaven departed as a scroll when it is rolled together; and every mountain and island were moved out of their places. / And the kings of the earth, and the great men, and the rich men, and the chief captains, and the mighty men, and every bondman, and every free man, hid themselves in the dens and in the rocks of the mountains; / And said to the mountains and rocks, Fall on us, and hide us from the face of him that sitteth on the throne, and from the wrath of the Lamb: / For the great day of his wrath is come; and who shall be able to stand?" (6:12-17).

The judgments described by the four horsemen are nothing compared to this last and final outpouring of the wrath of God. We will have occa-

sion to see the fury of this final judgment in greater
detail in subsequent scenes in this Apocalypse.
Here we have only a brief preview as a means
of comfort and consolation to those who were suffering at the hands of satanic persecutions.

Some think that this is only another picture depicting the instruments of judgment in the hands
of our God. In such a case this would be a picture
of judgment from natural calamity. We would not
say that this is an impossible interpretation, but
everything about this picture seems to point to
the final judgment. If we think that the judgments
of God are severe as they are now expressed, what
will we think when the day of his wrath is come?
The present judgments will seem as mere pin-
pricks in comparison to the utter devastation of
that final day of judgment.

In this instance the interlude between the sixth
and seventh symbols is an explanation. John antic-
ipated a question in the minds of his readers and
answered that question with an apocalyptic vision. It would perhaps be more accurate to say
that God answered this question by giving to John
another apocalyptic vision.

If such things as invasion, war, famine, and pestilence are instruments of God's judgment upon
the world, how is it that Christians are caught
up in these judgments the same as the unbelievers?
How can they be judgments if they fall upon the
redeemed the same as they fall upon the wicked?
This is the question which God answers in this
interlude. There is a twofold answer, and if we

study the vision carefully we will see that answer
in both parts.

John sees four angels standing on the four cor-
ners of the earth (the four points of the compass),
holding in their hands the four winds of judgment
as depicted in the vision of the four horsemen.
They are prepared to turn these winds loose upon
the earth. But before they turn them loose, another
angel ascends from the east and commands the
four angels "to hold their fire" until all of the servants of God had been sealed in their foreheads
with the seal which he carried in his hands. Thus
were the winds of judgment held back until every
believer had been properly sealed and identified.

Among those sealed were 144,000 from the
twelve tribes of Israel, 12,000 from each tribe.
Some have insisted on making this number literal,
thus concluding that only 144,000 Jews will be
saved. But in order to be consistent we look upon
this number as symbolic, along with the other
numbers used in the book of Revelation. This number is a multiple of twelve, which itself is the product of four, the earth number—times three, the
divine number, thus symbolizing God's divine plan
in his universe. The raising of the number to
144,000 is simply for emphasis. Whatever the actual number of Jews in the redeemed community
of heaven, it will be complete from the standpoint
of God's eternal purpose. Besides these 144,000
from the twelve tribes of Israel, John saw an innumerable host of others in the camp of the redeemed in glory. It is useless for us to speculate

on how many people will be saved.

The purpose of this phase of our vision is not that we might be given some indication of the number of the redeemed, but to show that before any wind of judgment is turned loose upon any part of our world, those who are to be redeemed will have been redeemed and properly identified. This, of course, introduces us to the subject of predestination, election, and foreordination, a subject which one runs into frequently as he reads through his New Testament. It is a subject which no human mind can completely comprehend. The great apostle Paul admitted that he did not understand it; yet he believed it. To the Romans he said: "O the depth of the riches both of the wisdom and knowledge of God! how unsearchable are his judgments, and his ways past finding out! / For who hath known the mind of the Lord? or who hath been his counsellor? / Or who hath first given to him, and it shall be recompensed unto him again? / For of him, and through him, and to him, are all things: to whom be glory for ever. Amen" (Rom. 11:33-36).

Once a young man went off to fight for his country in war. He was not a Christian. In a little time the report came that this young man had been killed in action. A friend made this remark: "This is so tragic. Just think, if he had not been killed in battle and could have come back home, he might have become a Christian!" We must admit that his death was tragic, but the subsequent statement has no scriptural justification. There is one thing sure: Had he been allowed to come back, he would not have become a Christian. Those who are chosen of God will respond to the call of God before some instrument of judgment strikes. This is the import of this vision, and it is verified and confirmed by other scriptural passages, such as Romans 8 and Ephesians 1.

The second comforting truth expressed in this vision is this: For those who have been thus redeemed, these instruments of judgment have no ill effect. What is a judgment to one man may be a benediction to another. These awesome acts of judgment described in the foregoing scenes are dreadful and disastrous upon the unbelievers, but they only serve to refine the life of the believer. Even if it should bring death, this is no catastrophe for the believer. On the contrary, it is the means by which God brings us into a better and sweeter life. Here is a fine Christian young man who must go out and fight for his country. The ravages of war fall upon him just as they fall upon the unbelievers. He dies along with the others, and our hearts sink in sorrow. The event is a tragedy and it does hurt, but for that young man this experience was no judgment of God upon him. It was simply God's way of bringing him into the blessedness of heavenly living. And if we could know just how blessed that life is, we would understand it better and would not look upon it as a tragedy.

This is the picture which John paints for his readers in the seventh chapter of the Revelation. Turning from these frightful pictures of judgment,

John is privileged to look out over the host of the
redeemed through that door into heaven. What
he saw was an inspiring sight—a multitude of
happy people, dressed in white robes, singing with
unexcelled joy. Presently one of the elders asked
in effect, "John, do you know who these are which
are robed in white and who sing with such joy?"
To this John replied by saying, "I don't know, but
surely you do. Please tell me." Then came the answer which must have thrilled the heart of that
aged saint as it did the persecuted Christians of
Asia when they first read it. "These are they which
came out of great tribulation, and have washed
their robes, and made them white in the blood
of the Lamb. / Therefore are they before the throne
of God, and serve him day and night in his temple:
and he that sitteth on the throne shall dwell among
them. / They shall hunger no more, neither thirst
any more; neither shall the sun light on them, nor
any heat. For the Lamb which is in the midst of
the throne shall feed them, and shall lead them
unto living fountains of waters: and God shall
wipe away all tears from their eyes" (7:14-17).

This is the picture which assured John and his
persecuted fellow Christians of Asia Minor that
no judgment or calamity, however severe, can really hurt the redeemed of God. Through these apparent judgments they enter into the fullness of
life in a blessed eternity. It should be noted that
these have come through "the great tribulation."
The article *does* appear with this term in the original language. Whatever is meant by this great

tribulation, these Christians had gone through it. They had not been raptured previously. Nor can we believe that this heavenly host represents only those who were converted during the tribulation period. John tells us that it was a numberless multitude.

This brings us to the opening of the seventh seal, which is transitional. When the seventh seal is loosed, there is a period of quiet for about the space of a half-hour. This period sets the stage for a series of seven trumpet blasts of warning. Looking back over this present series, we see a God of righteous judgment who judges this earth with his vehicles of wrath in just retribution; but in it all he makes ample provision for the safety and comfort of his own redeemed children. Furthermore, he gives ample warning to all before he strikes with these judgments, as we shall see in the next series of symbols.

CHAPTER SIX

The Timely Warnings
(8:6 to 11:19)

In the first episode we were privileged to see God on his throne in sovereignty and majesty with the worthy Lamb by his side. In the second episode we were privileged to see that this sovereign God is a God of righteous judgment. In this third episode we are to see that this God of righteous judgment does not strike with the full force of his wrath in judgment until he has given ample warning to all concerned. Thus we are able to see the logical development of this drama of redemption.

The scholars have varying ideas as to the chief significance of this series of symbols, but it seems to me that everything in this division of the book points to the idea of warning. We must admit that some of the details in the symbolism are far from clear, but that the overall emphasis is that of warning no honest student can deny. Each symbol in the series is introduced by the blast of a trumpet. The trumpet has long been used as an instrument of warning. Since the very earliest days it was used to alert soldiers to the approach of the enemy. Paul referred to it as such an instrument in his 1 Corinthian epistle: "For if the trumpet give an un-

certain sound, who shall prepare himself to the
battle?" (14:8). The recurrence of the trumpet
sound throughout leads rather impressively to
the conclusion that God is speaking here of the
methods by which he warns all men of his impending judgments. These are not pictures of judgments, but warnings of approaching judgments.

There are also other indications pointing to this
same conclusion. After six of these trumpet blasts
John explains that, in spite of these warnings, the
people "repented not of the works of their hands"
(9:20), thus indicating that they did not respond
to the warning. The interlude, as we shall see later,
also tells of announcements, prophesying, and witnessing. These are all expressions of warning. Let
us, therefore, approach this division of the Apocalypse with the understanding that these symbols
have something to do with the way in which God
warns men of his righteous judgments.

Just how does God go about the business of
warning men of his righteous judgments which are
destined to fall upon all evil? There are seven
trumpet blasts, and with each blast of the trumpet
we see a picture of warning. The first four depict
warning through nature. They describe natural calamities as a means of warning. In each case only
one-third of the earth is affected. These are what
we might call partial judgments, but they are designed as instruments of warning. The implication
is that each calamity covering one-third of the
earth is a warning to the remaining two-thirds.
Four great catastrophes in nature are described.

At the sound of the first angel, "there followed hail and fire mingled with blood, and they were cast upon the earth; and the third part of trees was burnt up, and all green grass was burnt up" (8:7). Here is a picture of a mighty hailstorm. The stones came down in the form of fire and clotted blood. They struck the earth with devastating effect. A third part of the vegetation was burned up and destroyed.

At the sound of the second trumpet, "as it were a great mountain burning with fire was cast into the sea; and the third part of the sea became blood; And the third part of the creatures which were in the sea, and had life, died; and the third part of the ships were destroyed" (8:8-9). Here is the picture of a mountain in volcanic eruption. It bursts forth into flames and is cast into the sea. A third part of the sea became blood as a third part of the life in it died.

When the third trumpet sounded, "there fell a great star from heaven, burning as it were a lamp, and it fell upon the third part of the rivers, and upon the fountains of waters; And the name of the star is called Wormwood: and the third part of the waters became wormwood; and many men died of the waters, because they were made bitter" (8:10-11). Here we have the picture of a gigantic comet hurtling through space. It fell upon the rivers and all freshwater supplies. The result was that a third part of the waters became bitter and many men died because of it. In John's day "Wormwood" was a substance known for its bitterness.

At the blast of the fourth trumpet, "the third part of the sun was smitten, and the third part of the moon, and the third part of the stars; so as the third part of them was darkened, and the day shone not for a third part of it, and the night likewise" (8:12). Here is the picture of a mighty eclipse. A third part of the sun was darkened, as was also a third part of the moon and the stars.

It is obvious that all four of these have to do with natural calamities; furthermore, each is partial, not total. This is one way that God warns all men. Every catastrophe in nature is but a sign from God to remind people everywhere that God does have such powers of destruction and that there is more of this to come. It should cause men to turn to God in repentance and faith. Reading of earthquakes, floods, tornadoes, and hurricanes should remind us of the awfulness of the judgment of God and cause us to think soberly of our relationship to him. This is a warning of a very general nature and is given to all men, regardless of location or rank in the world.

It was this kind of warning which led the apostle Paul to declare that even the Gentiles were without excuse before God. To the Romans he explained it like this: "For the wrath of God is revealed from heaven against all ungodliness and unrighteousness of men, who hold the truth in unrighteousness; / Because that which may be known of God is manifest in them; for God hath shewed it unto them. For the invisible things of him from the creation of the world are clearly seen, being understood by the things that are made, even his eternal power and Godhead; so that they are without excuse" (Rom. 1:18-20).

The fifth trumpet blast introduces us to a different kind of warning. John saw a star fall from heaven. To this star was given the key to the bottomless pit; and when he had opened this abyss, out came smoke which filled the air so that the sun was darkened by its presence. Out of the smoke came a great horde of locusts, but these were no ordinary locusts. They were in shape like horses prepared for battle, with faces like men and hair like women. They wore golden crowns upon their heads, and their teeth were like the teeth of lions. The flapping of their wings sounded like many horses running to battle. Their tails were like scorpions, and with these tails they could sting. They were not able to kill, but they were able to torment and make men wish they could die. They were able to inflict their torments only upon those who had not the seal of God in their foreheads.

The picture is a weird one, but not without significance. The fact that these inflictors of torment came forth from the pit of Satan himself, and that their work of torment was limited to the unbelievers or unregenerate, leads to the conclusion that this is some kind of warning which comes from within the kingdom of evil itself and is perpetrated by those who are associated with it. The symbolism must point to internal confusion and decadence within the wicked empire. The principle is applicable to any generation, for it has been true all through history; but for John and his Christian friends of Asia, this must have pointed to the godless empire of Rome. Whether or not they were conscious of it, forces of internal strife and decadence were already at work in the Roman Empire at the time John wrote. The Roman leaders were no doubt aware of them. The presence of such internal strife within any wicked regime is a warning from God. It indicates that that way of life is doomed for failure. The wise should take heed.

When the sixth angel sounded his trumpet, John heard a voice coming from the direction of the four horns of the golden altar. This voice tells the angel to "loose the four angels which are bound in the great river Euphrates" (9:14). When these were loosed there came forth an army of horsemen, 200,000,000 of them. The heads of the horses were like the heads of lions, and they belched out of their mouths fire, smoke, and brimstone. Their tails were like serpents. One-third of the men were killed by this invading horde of horses with their riders.

What is John trying to say to us here in this symbolic picture? Two things we know for sure— the picture is not a literal one, and it has something to do with warning. Beyond this we must tread with a somewhat uncertain step. Those who view this whole apocalyptic vision as a history of the church see in this symbolism a reference to the Mohammedan armies which invaded Palestine and parts of Asia Minor in the fourteenth and fif-

teenth centuries. Those who hold this view include
such men as Ellicott,[1] Barnes,[2] Mauro,[3] and, more
recently, Justin A. Smith.[4] It may be possible to
make such an application of the principle; but as
far as John and his readers were concerned, it
would make more sense to let the horsemen in
the vision refer to the Parthian horsemen who did
live in the Euphrates region and did come time
and again to inflict heavy damage upon the eastern
part of the Roman Empire. If this be true, the symbolic reference is the same as that conveyed by
the white horse and its rider in the sixth chapter.

Be that as it may, the principle expressed in
this imagery seems to be this: God warns a wicked
nation through damaging invasions by other nations. Leon Morris agrees that "as before, a third
must be taken as indicating a large number, but
not a majority. It is a warning to the rest to repent,
but John sadly records that they did not." [5] This
was certainly true of the great Roman Empire. The
Parthians never conquered Rome, but they did
come from time to time to inflict heavy damage.
These invasions were but forewarnings.

Thus do we have in these six symbols three
types of warning: natural calamity, internal decadence, and foreign invasion. In these three ways
God warns wicked nations and people of his impending judgments. These are all partial judgments, but a partial judgment is always a warning.
Well do I remember that when my mother would
chastise me lightly, she would always say something like, "Remember, son, there is much more

of this to come if you persist in doing wrong."
This is what God says to us through these partial
judgments. It is interesting to note that in Gibbon's
famous and classic history, the infidel historian
enumerates three great contributing causes of the
fall of the great Roman Empire.[6] They were (1) a
series of natural catastrophes; (2) internal corruption among the leaders; and (3) a series of foreign
invasions. This historical account fits the pattern
which is suggested by the imagery of the Apocalypse.

If God did nothing more than this, he would
be absolutely just and fair. He is under no obliga-
tion to give further warning. Such warnings have
been given to all peoples of all times in sufficient
measure. But our God is also loving and merciful.
He has gone the second and the third mile in his
effort to warn men of impending doom because
of sin. In the interlude between the sixth and the
seventh symbol in this series God shows, through
the apostle, how he does go the second mile in
the matter of warning. This is the longest of the
interludes and is probably the most difficult from
the standpoint of interpretation. Some aspects of
it are extremely nebulous; therefore, we will re-
frain from being too dogmatic. This much we do
know—that the total picture speaks of warning
and that this warning is felt at a more personal
nature than that which is pictured in the first six
symbols.

The central idea seems to be that of personal
witnessing to the men of earth concerning the judg-

ments of God against sin. In John's giving to us
this picture of personal witnessing, several figures
or symbols are brought into play. The interlude
(chaps. 10—11) opens with the coming of a mighty
angel from heaven who sets one foot upon the
sea and the other upon the land. He was clothed
with a cloud, and a rainbow was round about his
head. His face was as the sun and his feet as
pillars of fire. In his hand he held a little book
which was opened. When he opened his mouth
to speak, seven thunders uttered their voices. Just
as John was about to write down what the thunders uttered, a voice from heaven spoke com-
manding him not to write. It is useless for us to
speculate on what was contained in these utter-
ances or why John was not permitted to record
them for us. The angel did raise his hand toward
heaven and declare that "there should be time
no longer" (10:6). Perhaps a more literal translation
would read "There shall be no more delay."

Those who take the futurist approach to the
book of Revelation place the appearance of this
angel near the midpoint in the seven-year period
of tribulation at the end of the age, and the words
of the angel are interpreted as an announcement
of the final consummation. But I am inclined to
think that we have a symbolic picture here of the
voice of conscience which speaks to man to tell
him that he is not here on earth forever. Thus
he is warned to make preparation for that which
is beyond time.

John is told by the voice which he heard from

heaven to go up to the angel and take the book from his hand. When John approached the mighty angel, he was told by the angel to take the book and to eat it up. The angel forewarns the seer that while it will be sweet as honey on his tongue, it will become sour and bitter in his stomach. When John devoured the book, he discovered that the angel's prophecy was exactly right. It was like a sugarcoated pill, sweet in the beginning but bitter in the end. Surely no one would think of this as a literal picture. John only ate the book symbolically in the vision. The incident was designed to express a lesson.

What the angel said to John as he ate the book throws light on the meaning of the symbol. These are his words: "Thou must prophesy again before many peoples, and nations, and tongues, and kings" (10:11). The eating of the book seems to symbolize the proclamation of the Word of God through preaching. The idea of it is at first pleasant and thrilling, but in the performance of this task one experiences many things which are bitter. The idea that God has chosen the preacher to proclaim his blessed Word is a most delightful thought; but standing before men to condemn their sins, to warn them of a judgment to come, and to see them turn away in unbelief is a bitter experience which tries the soul. Nevertheless, it must be done in order that all men might be properly warned.

In pursuance of this responsibility, John is told by the angel to take a rod and measure the temple and the altar, but to pay no attention to the outer

court, for it had been given over to the Gentiles.
Just what was intended by this measuring of the
temple is not at all clear. It seems to be related
to the preceding symbol of the eating of the little
book and the prophesying to the nations. In thus
measuring the temple John discovers that there
is ample room and provision for the people of God
and that the Gentile unbelievers may come close,
but they can never enter the temple or expel the
people of God from it. The reference here to "Gentiles" seems to be a reference to unbelievers rather
than Gentile believers. It is so used on numerous
occasions in the New Testament. These unbelievers may even trample underfoot the holy city, but
for a limited time only, forty and two months (three
and one-half years—one-half of seven, the perfect
number). The futurists, of course, interpret this
scene literally, making it refer to that which will
take place in the rebuilt Temple in Jerusalem during the first half of the tribulation period.

Without interruption God proceeds to illustrate
this principle for John in a more personal way.
John sees two witnesses who go up and down
the land giving forth the prophecies of God with
great power for three and one-half years. Here
is the picture as John paints it for us. "And I will
give power unto my two witnesses, and they shall
prophesy a thousand two hundred and threescore
days, clothed in sackcloth. / These are the two
olive trees, and the two candlesticks standing before the God of the earth. / And if any man will
hurt them, fire proceedeth out of their mouth, and

devoureth their enemies; and if any man will hurt them, he must in this manner be killed. / These have power to shut heaven, that it rain not in the days of their prophecy; and have power over waters to turn them to blood, and to smite the earth with all plagues, as often as they will. / And when they shall have finished their testimony, the beast that ascendeth out of the bottomless pit shall make war against them, and shall overcome them, and kill them. / And their dead bodies shall lie in the street of the great city, which spiritually is called Sodom and Egypt, where also our Lord was crucified. / And they of the people and kindreds and tongues and nations shall see their dead bodies three days and an half, and shall not suffer their dead bodies to be put in graves. / And they that dwell upon the earth shall rejoice over them, and make merry, and shall send gifts one to another; because these two prophets tormented them that dwelt on the earth. / And after three days and an half the Spirit of life from God entered into them, and they stood upon their feet; and great fear fell upon them which saw them. / And they heard a great voice from heaven saying unto them, Come up hither. And they ascended up to heaven in a cloud; and their enemies beheld them. / And the same hour was there a great earthquake and the tenth part of the city fell, and in the earthquake were slain of men seven thousand: and the remnant were affrighted, and gave glory to the God of heaven" (11:3-13).

Much controversy has been waged over the

identity of these two witnesses. They have been
identified with many different persons and things.
Here are only a few of the theories proposed: The
Old and New Testaments; the Christian church
and the Christian state; Christ and John the Baptist; Saint Francis and Saint Dominic; John Huss
and Luther; the law and the gospel; Jew and Gentile Christians; the written Word and the spoken
Word; Moses and Elijah; Enoch and Elijah. Most
futurists hold that these two witnesses point to
two literal persons who are yet to appear on this
earth just before the consummation of the age.

In order to understand the basic import of the
lesson involved here, it is not necessary that these
two witnesses be identified with any specific person or thing. In fact, it is doubtful that John had
in mind here any particular person or persons.
The number two was selected because it represents that which confirms or verifies. Two witnesses are enough to give attestation to a fact;
yet they do not represent a great number or a
majority. This is a most appropriate image to represent the Christian witness in the world. It has
always been represented by a comparatively
small number. At times it has been represented
with great power and effectiveness; at other times
it has almost vanished from view. Here we have
a true picture of the Christian witness in the world.
There have been times when it has all but been
obliterated from the earth, but God has always
raised up other witnesses to continue the ministry
of warning to every evil and adulterous genera-

tion. The Christian witness has never been without opposition. The forcefulness of this opposition has fluctuated from generation to generation. If the Communists have their way, these witnesses will be killed; and over their dead bodies the people will rejoice.

Some will object to this interpretation by pointing out that nothing has ever happened in history like that described by John in this picture. The phenomena surrounding these two witnesses has not been seen in history. Therefore, it must refer to something which is yet in the future. With this conclusion we would have to agree if the picture painted here by John is a literal one. However, if the picture is figurative or symbolic, then it could very well serve to describe conditions which have existed and will exist in the history of redemption. Why must we insist on the literalness of this picture when most of the other pictures in the book of Revelation are admittedly symbolic?

In John's vision these dead bodies were left in the street of the great city, "which spiritually is called Sodom and Egypt." The qualifying phrase "where also our Lord was crucified" seems to point to Jerusalem. This could very well be the case, but if he is speaking "spiritually," this could be a reference to Rome; and I am inclined to think so. Was it not from Rome that the authority came for the crucifixion of our Lord? Perhaps it was put like this in order to circumvent the Roman censors. To what exact city the reference points is secondary. The basic principle is that God's witnesses in the world have from time to time been squelched and even killed in the citadels of wickedness, but God has raised up these witnesses time and again to continue this ministry of warning and evangelization in the world. No one will ever be able to point an accusing finger into the face of God and say that he was not properly warned.

In spite of all these warnings in all these forms, the great masses of the people did not repent or turn to the Lord in submissive faith. The sad story is told in the last two verses of the ninth chapter. "And the rest of the men which were not killed by these plagues yet repented not of the works of their hands, that they should not worship devils, and idols of gold, and silver, and brass, and stone, and of wood: which neither can see, nor hear, nor walk: Neither repented they of their murders, nor of their sorceries, nor of their fornication, nor of their thefts" (vv. 20-21).

Because of this failure to respond to the warning, there must be the inevitable conflict between the forces of God's righteous judgments and the forces of evil. Thus the battle begins to shape up, and the stage has been set for a terrific conflict which will unfold before our eyes in the next episode. The sounding of the seventh trumpet issues in a transitional picture. It declares the assured victory of the redeemed. John heard a great heavenly choir singing, "The kingdoms of this world are become the kingdoms of our Lord, and of his Christ; and he shall reign for ever and ever"

(11:15). This is the positive side of this picture of warning. Those who heed the warning can be assured of glorious victory. This also gives a brief hint of the great conflict which is upcoming in our next series of symbols.

CHAPTER SEVEN

The Inevitable Conflict
(12:1 to 14:20)

In spite of all the warnings from a just and righteous God, the masses of men did not repent or turn to God in faith. Therefore, the conflict is inevitable. Since men will not repent, there must be a head-on collision between the righteousness of God and the wickedness of men. Thus has the stage been set for the conflict of the ages. Everything in this section speaks of conflict. The battle lines are drawn up; the opposing commanders appear with their forces; and skirmishes are already taking place. The seven images or figures are not as clearly marked in numerical order as in the foregoing series of symbols with the seven trumpeters, but seven images do appear on the scene as one examines the content of these chapters.

Some highly regarded Bible scholars think that chapter 12 marks the dividing line between the two main divisions of the book—the first revealing Christ as head of the church and the controller of the destiny of the world, and the second revealing the trials and triumphs of the church. This is the view of H. B. Swete.[1] Others, like R. C. H. Lenski,[2] recognize these same two divisions but believe that the two divisions tell the same story in its entirety but with a different set of symbols. Others look upon the first division (chaps. 4—11) as a picture of events which will take place during the first three and one-half years of the seven-year period of tribulation at the end of the age, and the second division as a picture of events which shall take place during the last three and one-half years of the tribulation period.

I see in this section a continuation of the story of redemption, showing another vital factor in the logical unfolding of the drama of redemption. It is the idea of conflict, and it follows in logical (but not chronological) order the series of symbols depicting warning. God warns; people do not give heed; the inevitable result is conflict. Here we see the occasion for the conflict, the opposing forces in battle array, and a brief preview of the outcome.

The first symbol which we see in this phase of the apocalyptic vision is a woman clothed with the sun and the moon under her feet. She wears on her head a diadem of twelve stars. All agree that this woman in the vision is symbolic in nature, but there are widely varying opinions as to what she symbolizes. The Roman Catholics insist that she represents Mary, the mother of Jesus. Others look upon her as a symbol of the church, but this would make the church as the producer of Christ instead of (as the New Testament seems to indicate) Christ producing the church. This is putting the cart before the horse. The dispensationalists insist that this woman symbolizes the nation of

Israel. This makes good sense except for the fact that her seed are pictured in 12:17 as those who "have the testimony of Jesus Christ." Leon Morris suggests that her symbolism changes in the development of the vision.[3] At first she represents Israel, but in the latter part of the chapter she represents the church. It seems to make better sense to say that she represents the chosen people of God. In the Old Testament these people were the Israelites, but in the New Testament they are the followers of Christ, the spiritual Israel.

The important thing to remember about this woman, whatever may be her proper identity, is that she is used here as a springboard to introduce the conflict. The occasion for this conflict had already been established in the preceding episode, when God showed the unwillingness of the people to repent in the face of many warnings. But now God is showing to us the more immediate cause of the conflict. In every conflict there are always the long-range causes which are at work under the surface for many years; then there are also the more immediate causes which precipitate the open hostilities. Here we see the cause of the conflict from a somewhat different point of view.

As the woman appears on the scene, she is about to give birth to a child. Soon the child is born—a man-child who is destined to rule the world with a rod of iron. Presently he is "caught up unto God, and to his throne" (12:5). In one little verse the whole span of the life of Jesus on earth is encompassed. He was born . . . and he was caught up. It was not necessary here to give more detail on the earthly life and ministry of our Lord. This had already been done in the Gospels; and, furthermore, it was not necessary in the light of the purpose of the Revelation to give us the larger and panoramic view of the total picture of God's redemptive program. It is quite clear, however, that the conflict wages around this child who was born and then caught up.

Almost simultaneously with the introduction of the woman who was about to give birth to the child, we are introduced to the commander in chief of the forces of evil. He is pictured as a great red dragon, so gigantic and mighty that with one swish of his tail he could knock down a third of the stars of the heavens. He had seven heads and ten horns, with a crown upon each head. This, of course, is not a literal picture of Satan. The seven heads speak of the fullness of evil; the crowns speak of his authority; and his great power is symbolized in the horns and the swishing of his tail. In verse 9 he is clearly identified as "the old serpent, called the Devil, and Satan, which deceiveth the whole world." There can be no doubt as to his identity. It is obvious that he is one who wishes to rule over all things and to keep them under his control.

Knowing that this man-child was destined to rule the nations, he waits to pounce on the little child as soon as he is born, to crush its life and thus win the crown for himself. But somehow God intervenes, protecting the child while he is here

and soon taking him into the safety of his own
heavenly kingdom. The old dragon is determined
not to be outdone, so he pursues the man-child
right on up to the gates of the heavenly city. There
a terrific conflict ensues. Michael and his angels
fight against the dragon and his angels. Michael
wins the struggle, and the old dragon loses his
foothold in heaven. He is cast back onto the earth,
but he is furious with rage because he has lost
this struggle.

Some think that they see here a picture of the
origin of Satan. There is some reason to believe
from inferences here and there in the Scripture
that Satan was once an angel in heaven who went
by the name of Lucifer (son of the morning, Isa.
14:12-17). Other passages which give veiled hints
are these: Ezekiel 28:15; 1 Timothy 3:6; John 8:44;
Jude 6. But it is not within the bounds of sound
exposition to build a whole theory of Satan's origin
on a few nebulous passages such as this one in
the book of Revelation. Furthermore, this could
not possibly be an account of Satan's origin, since
it follows the birth and ascension of Jesus Christ.
Satan had been at work on this earth long before
that.

Neither can this be a picture of the final struggle
between God and Satan at the close of the seven-
year period of tribulation, as claimed by the futurists, for after this incident Satan returns to earth
to enter into a seemingly long conflict with the
remnant of the woman's seed who have "the testimony of Jesus" (v. 17). It simply shows the immedi-

ate occasion for the conflict which is being experienced by the people of God and the forces of evil on this earth, past, present, and future. Let us remember that even though John saw all of this drama through the open door into heaven, this is not to say that everything he saw actually took place within the confines of the heavenly abode of the saints. The impression which comes to my mind as I read the story is simply this: Satan was so intent upon capturing Jesus and crushing out his life that he pursued him to the very door of heaven, and there the struggle took place. *The New English Bible* seems to imply as much in its translation of this passage: "Then war broke out in heaven. Michael and his angels waged war upon the dragon. The dragon and his angels fought, but they had not the strength to win, and no foothold was left them in heaven. So the great dragon was thrown down" (12:7-8). "Thrown down" seems to be a better translation of the original language here than "cast out." The dramatic element is predominant in the picture.

The devil knew that the key to victory in overcoming the forces of righteousness was in the crushing of the life of the incarnate Son of God; therefore, he gave his paramount effort toward the reaching of this goal. When he was unable to crush and destroy the life of the Son of God, the victory was assured for the people of God, though the battle was by no means over. It was through the very blood which Satan was able to draw from the life of this man-child that he lost the struggle.

This is the paradox of all ages. Just as Satan was about to rejoice over what he thought to be a tremendous triumph for him, Jesus broke loose from the bonds of death to glorious life. Suddenly Satan realized that he had not won the victory at all. He became furious and enraged. Through all the struggle down through the ages the secret or key to victory is the blood of Christ. "And they overcame him by the blood of the Lamb, and by the word of their testimony; and they loved not their lives unto the death" (12:11).

The third image in this series reveals to us the object of Satan's anger in the world today—the remnant of the woman's seed. Having become enraged by his failure to crush the life of the man-child, Satan returns to the earth with a mad passion to destroy the woman who gave birth to the child and her seed. These are identified as those who have "the testimony of Jesus" (12:17). There is no doubt about it; the devil is intent upon hurting and destroying the people of God and their witness to Jesus. The symbolism is dramatic. "And when the dragon saw that he was cast unto the earth, he persecuted the woman which brought forth the man child. / And to the woman were given two wings of a great eagle, that she might fly into the wilderness, into her place, where she is nourished for a time, and times, and half a time, from the face of the serpent. / And the serpent cast out of his mouth water as a flood after the woman, that he might cause her to be carried away of the flood. / And the earth helped the woman, and the earth opened her mouth, and swallowed up the flood which the dragon cast out of his mouth. / And the dragon was wroth with the woman, and went to make war with the remnant of her seed, which keep the commandments of God, and have the testimony of Jesus Christ" (12:13-17).

The futurists see here a picture of Israel as a nation as she is protected and preserved from destruction by the enemy during the last half of the seven-year tribulation period at the end of the age. We are told that she "is nourished for a time, and times, and half a time." This is three and one-half, but let us not forget that we are dealing with symbols. The three and one-half is symbolic of that which is incomplete or temporary, one-half of the complete number, seven. To make it refer to a literal three and one-half years at the end of the age creates an untenable situation in the interpretation of the verses which follow, for it is after this period that the devil will make war with the remnant of her seed, those who have the testimony of Jesus. The picture which John seems to be painting here is simply this: Having failed in his effort to crush out the life of the Son of God, the devil has set himself to do all the damage he can to the followers of Jesus, from the first generation on down to the present one. True believers in Christ are the objects of Satan's wrath, and against them he constantly wages war.

Having been introduced to the commander in chief of the forces of evil and having seen some-

thing of his purpose and plan in the earth, we
are now ready to meet his right-hand man, his
secretary of war. He is described as a beast who
rises up out of the sea. He has seven heads and
ten horns. Upon each horn is a crown, and upon
his heads the name of blasphemy. This beast was
like a leopard; yet he had feet like a bear and a
mouth like a lion. He received his power and authority from the old dragon. The people bowed
down before him and worshiped him. He was
given power to continue for forty-two months—
that is, three and one-half years, which is one-
half of the complete number, seven. As in previous
instances, we see here not a literal period of three
and one-half years, but a period of limited or incomplete time.

This beast makes war against those who have
the seal of God in their foreheads. He is indignant
against these because they will not fall down and
worship him. How shall we identify this beast in
the symbolism? Some think that he represents a
great and last godless world political leader, the
Antichrist, who is yet to appear on the scene. I
would agree that in principle he represents any
powerful godless political leader or world power;
but as far as John and his fellow Christians of
the first century were concerned, he was none
other than Domitian, the blasphemous emperor of
Rome. John is careful thus to identify him. He gives
a very strong clue. One of the heads of the beast
was "as it were wounded to death; and his deadly
wound was healed; and all the world wondered

after the beast" (13:3). It was commonly believed by many of the people of John's day that Domitian was the reincarnation of Nero. We will have occasion to say more about this when we come to another description of this beast in the seventeenth chapter. Suffice it to say here that John, of course, did not believe this legend; but he used it to identify the beast for his readers. Indeed, he was the earthly leader of the forces of wickedness in that day, and the Christians of John's day recognized him as such. The principle may be appropriately applied to any godless dictator of any generation. For us today it could be the blasphemous leadership of Communist Russia.

The fifth symbol in this series introduces us to the third in command of the forces of evil in the world. He is the field general. He is described as a second beast, but he is unlike the first beast in that he has two horns like a lamb. But he gets his power from the first beast. He spends his time out among the people getting them to bow down before the image of the first beast and seeing to it that the people follow the decrees of this first beast. He has a pleasant first appearance and is able to perform apparent miracles, even to the making of the image of the first beast to talk. He sees to it that no one can buy or sell who does not have the mark of the beast in his right hand or on his forehead.

Some have identified this second beast with false religion. This would mean that the opposers of Christianity in the world are outspoken political

dictators and deceiving religious leaders. We
would have to admit that this is often true; but
if we understand the mind of the apostle, he must
have been thinking of the officers of the Roman
government who worked under the direction of
the emperor. Perhaps the reference was to the Roman governors of the provinces, called the com-
munes, whose responsibility it was to carry out
the edicts of the emperor. There is nothing in the
picture here to indicate that this second beast was
a religious leader, even though John does refer
to him in 16:13 as "the false prophet." He is simply
the assistant of the first beast. Again we must
say that the principle may be applied to the godless assistants of the godless dictators in any generation; but as far as John and his readers were
concerned, he was none other than the Roman
commune who inflicted the wishes of the emperor
upon the people.

For the comfort of his readers, John further identifies the beast by giving to him a number which
symbolizes a blessed truth. The number is 666.
Through the years Bible students have labored
long in trying to figure out the significance of this
number. The results have been fantastic. Some
have worked out intricate and complicated
schemes by giving numerical value to the letters
of the Hebrew or Greek alphabet, depending upon
their position. Then they would add up the numerical value of certain outstanding names until they
arrived at the total of 666. Some came out with
the name of Nero Caesar, others with the name

Lateinos. Such a system of interpretation borders on the ridiculous. We have neither time nor disposition to review all of these attempts at interpretation.

The simple and obvious meaning is this: The number six is just short of the complete and perfect number seven. It no doubt refers to that which is powerful but short of perfect—therefore, doomed to ultimate failure. The repeating of the number three times is for the sake of emphasis. Six hundred and sixty-six is more emphatic than six. What John is trying to say is simply this: These forces of evil headed up by the dragon, the first beast, and the second beast are impressive and powerful, but ultimately they will fall. That is why John prefaces his reference to this number of the beast with these words: "Here is wisdom. Let him that hath understanding count the number of the beast: for it is the number of a man; and his number is Six hundred threescore and six" (13:18).

The sixth image in this series turns our attention to the other side of the battlefield. There on a small hill called mount Sion stood a Lamb with 144,000 of his devoted followers. Just as Babylon was a symbol of the citadel of wickedness, so has Sion stood through the years as a symbol of the citadel of God's righteousness. Here on mount Sion we see this Lamb, and we recognize him as the same Lamb who appeared on the heavenly scene in the first episode to take the sealed scroll out of the hand of him who sat upon the throne. The 144,000 are the redeemed out of the earth.

Some insist that this figure must be taken literally; but, just as in the seventh chapter, we take this number to be symbolic of the redeemed. The 144,000 is a multiple of twelve, the number which symbolizes God's full manifestation on the earth through his divinely appointed institutions. Let us say, therefore, that this number represents a full manifestation of God's redeemed people as they carry out the plan and purpose of God on earth. Actually, it is a small number when compared to the innumerable masses fighting under the banner of the dragon. These who stand with the Lamb on mount Sion are not sad; neither are they weeping. They are singing a new song, and it is a song of victory.

These are described as "they which were not defiled with women; for they are virgins" (14:4). It should be remembered that this is figurative language, not literal. If this were literal, it would mean that no married people would be among the redeemed. This is ridiculous. What John means is that these redeemed were people who had proved true to the Lamb and had not been guilty of spiritual adultery.

The interlude between the sixth and seventh symbols introduces us to three angels who swoop down over the battlefield to make announcements. Already there are skirmishes in the valley. Blood has already been shed, and it appears that there is little hope for the outnumbered followers of the Lamb. But as John looks upon this scene he sees three angels in flight. The first one John describes as follows: "And I saw another angel fly in the midst of heaven, having the everlasting gospel to preach unto them that dwell on the earth, and to every nation, and kindred, and tongue, and people, / Saying with a loud voice, Fear God, and give glory to him; for the hour of his judgment is come; and worship him that made heaven, and earth, and the sea, and the fountains of waters" (14:6-7).

As the climax of the battle approached, God gave one more opportunity for the men in Satan's army to repent and turn to God. This angel represents the messengers of God, who continue to warn men and plead with them to turn from their sins to God. The door is not yet closed. There is still time and opportunity for men to flee from the wrath to come.

The second angel swooped down over the battlefield and announced the fall of the citadel of wickedness. "And there followed another angel, saying, Babylon is fallen, is fallen, that great city, because she made all nations drink of the wine of the wrath of her fornication" (v. 8). So sure was he of the final outcome that he could announce it as if it were already a reality. The Christians of Asia Minor surely recognized in this a prophecy of the downfall of the wicked city of Rome. As we have noted previously, Babylon is the symbol of any citadel of wickedness.

The third angel appeared over the battlefield to give one last word of warning and encouragement to the struggling saints in the valley of conflict. Even though it may have appeared to be a losing battle at the moment, nothing would have been gained by compromising with the dragon and his beast. There is an earnest appeal for steadfastness on the part of the redeemed. Those who default to the beast will drink of the wine of the wrath of God. In fact, said the angel, it is far better to die in the struggle than to bow down for one minute to the beast or his image. The words of the inspired apostle here are among the sweetest and most comforting words in all Scripture: "And the third angel followed them, saying with a loud voice, If any man worship the beast and his image, and receive his mark in his forehead, or in his hand, / The same shall drink of the wine of the wrath of God which is poured out without mixture into the cup of his indignation; and he shall be tormented with fire and brimstone in the presence of the holy angels, and in the presence of the Lamb: / And the smoke of their torment ascendeth up for ever and ever: and they have no rest day nor night, who worship the beast and his image, and whosoever receiveth the mark of his name. / Here is the patience of the saints: here are they that keep the commandments of God, and the faith of Jesus. / And I heard a voice from heaven saying unto me, Write, Blessed are the dead which die in the Lord from henceforth; Yea, saith the Spirit, that they may rest from their labours; and their works do follow them" (14:9-13).

The seventh symbol comes to us in the form of a sickle and is transitional. It prepares us for the next series of symbols which speak of God's final judgment upon the world. The symbol of the sickle is doubled for emphasis. The sickle first appeared in the hand of one who sits upon a cloud. An angel appeared, calling for this one who sits upon the cloud to put in his sickle and reap the harvest. In reply to the angel's voice, he thrust in his sharp sickle, and the earth was reaped. The second time the sickle appeared in the hands of an angel. Another angel called for him to put in his sharp sickle, and this he did. Here we have a picture of the climax and consummation of the battle between the forces of evil and the forces of God. The end is in sight; the harvest is about to be reaped. Here is a foregleam of that climax which will be given in greater detail as the seven angels pour out their seven bowls of wrath. It is a picture of utter devastation. "And the angel thrust in his sickle into the earth, and gathered the vine of the earth, and cast it into the great winepress of the wrath of God. / And the winepress was trodden without the city, and blood came out of the winepress, even unto the horse bridles, by the space of a thousand and six hundred furlongs" (14:19-20).

CHAPTER EIGHT
The Decisive Climax
(15—16)

Sovereignty, judgment, warning, and conflict—
these are the major factors in the unfolding drama
of redemption as seen from John's vantage point,
looking through that open door into heaven. In
the fourth act of the drama we saw the opposing
forces lined up in battle array. We saw something
of the occasion of the conflict, the principal partici-
pants in the conflict, and something of the fierceness of it. We come now to the climax of this
great conflict. Many skirmishes have already
taken place in the valley, but now we are privileged to see through the eyes of John this conflict
in its climactic consummation, when God delivers
his "Sunday punch."

This climax of the battle comes to us in the
form of seven bowls of wrath, which are poured
out by seven angels from the portals of heaven.
We are first introduced to these in the fifteenth
chapter, which opens with this description by
John: "And I saw another sign in heaven, great
and marvellous, seven angels having the seven
last plagues; for in them is filled up the wrath of
God" (15:1). We have already been given several

foregleams of this climactic event, but now we are about to see it in all of its fullness. Even before the contents of the bowls of wrath are poured out, John gives another little foregleam of the final victory. Along with the seven angels with the seven bowls John "saw as it were a sea of glass mingled with fire; and them that had gotten the victory over the beast, and over his image, and over his mark, and over the number of his name, stand on the sea of glass, having the harps of God. / And they sing the song of Moses the servant of God, and the song of the Lamb, saying, Great and marvellous are thy works, Lord God Almighty; just and true are thy ways, thou King of saints. / Who shall not fear thee, O Lord, and glorify thy name? For thou only art holy; for all nations shall come and worship before thee; for thy judgments are made manifest" (15:2-4).

As John continues to look through that open door into heaven, he sees seven angels coming out of the temple in heaven. So austere is the sight that smoke fills the temple, and no one is able to go in or out until the seven angels had dispatched their bowls of wrath. A voice out of the temple commanded these angels to go forth and pour out their bowls of wrath upon the earth. Judgments of God are expressed all along, but there came a time in the conflict between the good and the evil when God said, "It is enough." Then God turned loose the full fury of his wrath in judgment.

A good illustration of this principle may be taken from World War II. Our men had been in

combat with the Japanese all through the South
Sea islands. These skirmishes were real battles,
sometimes in favor of our soldiers and sometimes
in favor of the Japanese. Finally our military leaders got together and said, "This has gone far
enough; we must now give them our 'Sunday
punch.'" Soon our planes dropped atomic bombs
on two great cities of Japan. There was never anything like it before. Those skirmishes in the South
Sea islands seemed as "play war" in comparison
to the utter devastation left by those atomic
bombs. This brought that terrible war to a climactic and victorious close.

War follows the same general pattern, whether
it is one nation fighting against another with
bombs and bullets or a struggle between good and
evil in a spiritual warfare. In the struggle between
the forces of righteousness and the forces of evil,
God is the commander in chief of the forces of
righteousness and Satan is the leader of the opposition. There will come a time in this warfare when
God will drop his atomic bomb and bring the conflict to a climactic close. In the sixteenth chapter
of the Revelation we have the picture of this climax in significant and forceful imagery. Let us
not forget that it is imagery and not a literal picture. The real thing must be much worse than the
image which is used to describe it.

As each angel stepped forward to empty his
bowl of wrath upon the earth, an aspect of this
climax could be seen. Seven signifies that this is
the full and complete expression of the wrath of

God against evil. It will be obvious to the reader of the Revelation that at the beginning of chapter 16 the action decidedly picks up momentum. Here the action gets fast and furious because we are approaching the climactic end. In fact, as one reads through the sixteenth chapter, he finds himself getting out of breath as he tries to keep up with the fast-moving actions. The emptying of the bowls is given in rapid succession.

The first four are related to natural calamity, and they correspond to the first four trumpet blasts in chapter 8. The first had its effect upon the earth; the second upon the sea; the third upon the fresh waters; and the fourth upon the sun, moon, and stars. However, there are two distinct differences. In the case of the trumpets, only a third was affected because these were partial judgments designed as instruments of warning to the two-thirds left. Here the judgment is full and final; therefore, the whole is affected. But there is still another difference. In the case of the trumpet blasts, both the good and the bad were caught up in the partial judgments. Here the judgments fall only on the unbelievers. The saints are snatched away and taken out of the line of fire as God's atomic bombs are turned loose. John explains that the first bowl of wrath was poured out upon the earth, and "there fell a noisome and grievous sore upon the men which had the mark of the beast, and upon them which worshipped his image" (16:2).

After the pouring out of the third bowl of wrath, John cannot contain himself. He just has to turn

aside for a moment to show what is going on in
heaven among the redeemed of God while the
bowls of wrath are being poured out. It is a scene
of ecstasy. "And I heard the angel of the waters
say, Thou art righteous, O Lord, which art, and
wast, and shalt be, because thou hast judged
thus. / For they have shed the blood of saints and
prophets, and thou hast given them blood to drink;
for they are worthy. And I heard another out of
the altar say, Even so, Lord God Almighty, true
and righteous are thy judgments" (16:5-7).

The redeemed with all of the hosts of heaven
will rejoice when they see these terrible plagues
falling upon those who had for so long been enemies of God and of his people. This is not to say
that any Christian should rejoice over the downfall
of any other individual no matter how wicked he
may have been; but when at the end of the age
we see the mighty judgments of a just God fall
upon the enemies of God and of righteousness,
we will have every reason to shout for joy. And
we shall. God will administer this righteous retribution in due time; and when he does, it will be
a cause of great rejoicing among the redeemed.

After this brief interruption during which the
hosts of heaven turned loose in a doxology of
praise to God, the fourth angel stepped forward
and emptied his bowl upon the sun so that the
heat thereof was intensified until it scorched all
these wicked men. Instead of repenting, they blasphemed the name of God.

What we have seen so far is only the first stage

of this atomic blast of God. There is more to come. The fifth angel poured out his bowl of wrath upon the seat of the beast, causing a complete blackout in the kingdom of the beast. The people gnawed their tongues in agony and blasphemed the God of heaven. The picture is a brief one, but its significance seems to be clear. It is a picture of judgment from internal decadence and corruption. The wicked kingdom is made to fall apart as a result of corruption from within. It is the same type of judgment which is depicted in the fifth trumpet blast of the ninth chapter. The difference is that in the earlier picture there is not power to kill but only to hurt for five months. There it is a picture of warning by partial judgment. Here the devastation is complete. It is judgment in its final form.

The sixth angel poured out his vial of wrath upon the great river Euphrates. The effect of this blast was that the water of the river was dried up, paving the way for the coming of the kings of the east. These kings are described in the ninth chapter as an army of two hundred million men riding on horses. In that instance they were given power to kill one-third of the men. Here there is no limitation placed upon them. As in the earlier case, here also the imagery seems to symbolize the idea of foreign invasion. For the wicked Roman Empire of the first century, this meant the invasion of the Parthians from the east. As we pointed out earlier, history records the fact that three major factors combined to bring the mighty Roman Empire to dissolution—a series of natural calamities, internal strife among the wicked leaders, and a series of foreign invasions. Thus John's picture of judgment fits into the historic record. However, the principle may be applied to any generation.

In the brief interlude between the sixth and seventh bowls of wrath, John gives us an interesting sidelight concerning the reaction of the godless empire to these mighty judgments. Just when it appears that the wicked kingdom is about to succumb to these mighty blasts from God's atomic arsenal, we see three slick, slimy frogs come forth out of the mouth of the dragon, the beast, and the false prophet (the second beast). These three frogs go forth up and down the land, seeking recruits for a great battle which is shaping up. It is referred to in our text as the battle of Armageddon, that great day of God Almighty.

Much has been said about this battle of Armageddon. The futurists especially have made much of it. They interpret it as being a literal struggle with the customary instruments of warfare at some future date in a particular spot in the land of Palestine. To be consistent, if one takes the reference to Armageddon literally, then he ought also to take the reference to the three slick, slimy frogs literally. Both references appear in the same passage; yet no one ever suggests that there will be three frogs literally going about over the earth seeking recruits for this battle. In order to follow the path of consistency, we choose to look upon this reference to Armageddon as symbolic imagery, as with the reference to the frogs.

Armageddon is actually a word which John coined. It literally means "the mount of Megiddo." The term Megiddo does appear in the Old Testament. It refers to a narrow strip of plain just south of Nazareth in Palestine. There is a mount overlooking this valley, which was also called the plain of Esdraelon. On this little mound can be seen the ruins of the ancient city of Megiddo. Many of the most decisive battles of Israel's history were fought in this plain of Megiddo. Here Deborah and Barak routed the forces of Sisera; here Saul and Jonathan fought their last battles with the Philistines; here Jehu staged his bloody revolution; here good king Josiah lost his life in a conflict with Pharaoh-Nechoh of Egypt. Thus through the years this plain of Megiddo became in the minds of the Jews a symbol of conflict or decisive battle. John no doubt used the word as a symbol of a place of decisive battle. He was not thinking of a literal battle to be fought with the earthly weapons of warfare at a literal place in the land of Palestine. W. Hendriksen is perhaps right in concluding that "Har-Megedon is the symbol of every battle in which, when the need is greatest and believers are oppressed, the Lord suddenly reveals his power in the interest of his distressed people and defeats the enemy." [1]

The true significance of this sign must be something like this: When God comes to unload the full fury of his wrath upon the satanic kingdom, Satan will do what any nation would do in the course of a battle. Let me illustrate from World

War II. After many skirmishes with the Germans all over Europe, the Allies decided that it was time to move against the enemy with all that they had. They stormed the mainland with the best of their troops and pushed the Germans back. Soon it was obvious to all, even to the enemy, that the Allies held the upper hand and victory was in sight. But just at that moment Hitler decided that he would make one more last-ditch, all-out stand, hoping against hope to turn the tide of battle. He put everything he had into the Battle of the Bulge, but it was not enough. He went down in ignominious defeat.

Just as the enemy always does when he sees the end in sight, the devil will make that one all-out, last-ditch stand, hoping to turn the tide of battle. This is the picture which John paints in this interlude. The old devil and his cohorts were reeling under the mighty blows of these atomic blasts from God's bowls of wrath, but the devil sent out his emissaries to recruit every possible soldier for one last stand. This is the battle of Armageddon.

The question invariably arises—when will this battle take place? As far as John and these first-century Christians were concerned, it took place when the mighty and blasphemous Roman Empire fell. For them this empire was the epitome of satanic power and wickedness. In this sense the battle of Armageddon was to them yet future; to us it is history. However, we must not stop here if we are to understand the full significance of this apocalyptic picture. This battle of Armageddon has been fought many times throughout history. It happens when any satanic power goes down in defeat and dissolution. It will happen again and again in the experience of future generations. And then it will happen in one gigantic Armageddon at the end of the age when all the combined forces of evil will fall into ignominious dissolution after one more great all-out effort to overcome the forces of righteousness.

Armageddon also happens to every individual in a personal sense. Every man's heart is an Armageddon, a battlefield in which the forces of evil and the forces of righteousness struggle against each other. And always when the devil sees that he is about to lose the battle, he makes that last big fling, hoping to turn the tide. Often when one is under conviction and about ready to make that decision to surrender to the lordship of Jesus Christ, the devil puts forth that extra effort, causing a temporary rebellion against God and all that is right. I have seen it happen many times; I have even experienced it in my own heart. These are Armageddon experiences. Albert H. Baldinger rightly observes that "there is a sense in which every man's life is a miniature Armageddon." [2] At least there are times when it becomes that.

Just when the devil thinks he may have a chance to turn the tide of battle, God comes with his last and fatal nuclear blast. The seventh angel stepped forward with his bowl of wrath and pours it out into the air. The effect is almost beyond human comprehension. The fact is that the human mind cannot now fully understand the full force and effect of this last bowl of wrath. John tries to describe it for us. What an awesome picture he presents! "And there were voices, and thunders, and lightnings; and there was a great earthquake, such as was not since men were upon the earth, so mighty an earthquake, and so great. / And the great city was divided into three parts, and the cities of the nations fell: / And great Babylon came in remembrance before God, to give unto her the cup of the wine of the fierceness of his wrath. / And every island fled away, and the mountains were not found. / And there fell upon men a great hail out of heaven, every stone about the weight of a talent: and men blasphemed God because of the plague of the hail; for the plague thereof was exceeding great" (16:18-21).

Through John God gave us a brief foreshadowing of this great and final judgment in the sixth chapter, but here we have it in all of its awful fullness. This time as the angel turned his bowl upside down, a great voice was heard out of the temple saying, "It is done." This is all of it, the final stroke from God's atomic arsenal. And it is sufficient. There is nothing left of the enemy. The destruction and devastation are complete. The enemy has been destroyed and his kingdom devastated. Babylon came in remembrance before God. This was no doubt a reference to Rome, the center and citadel of the wicked kingdom as John and his Christian friends knew it. But it is also a symbol of any similar seat of wickedness.

This last symbol of judgment takes us, of course, into that which is yet future: how far into the future we would not dare to speculate. We only know that in the consummation of the age, God will bring to bear such tremendous judgment force that every vestige of evil will be wiped from the face of the earth, and with it will come complete and final victory to the redeemed of God. When the smoke of this last atomic blast has cleared away, we will be able to survey the battleground to see the completeness of the destruction of evil and the victory of righteousness. This will issue in a never-to-be-forgotten series of celebrations, which we will be privileged to see in the next series of symbols.

CHAPTER NINE

The Celestial Celebration
(17:1 to 20:10)

It is always customary for the victor to celebrate when the battle is over. In the last episode, as described by John from his vantage point at the door of heaven, we saw the climax of the mighty struggle between the forces of righteousness and the forces of evil. God came with his seven bowls of wrath and brought utter devastation to the forces of evil. The smoke of battle has now cleared away, and we are ready to see something of the completeness of the victory for the saints of God and the program of celebration which followed.

As in all the foregoing episodes, there are seven symbols with an interlude between the sixth and the seventh. In this instance, as in the case of the episode describing the opposing forces in battle array (chaps. 12—14), the divisions are not clearly numbered, but they will be obvious to the careful reader. There are seven scenes of celebration with a special feature of the celebration described in the interlude. Everything within this section of the Apocalypse bears the mark of celebration, which is a logical sequence to the climax of the battle.

The first feature of the celebration is more or less introductory and designed to identify the conquered enemy. In this first scene God is very careful to identify the conquered enemy. He wants his redeemed people, especially the persecuted Christians of Asia Minor, to understand who has thus been conquered and destroyed. The whole of the seventeenth chapter is occupied with this picture of identity. One of the angels who had one of the seven bowls of wrath is about to take John on a tour of the enemy territory so that he might rejoice in the completeness of the victory, but first he must identify this enemy and his territory. So he carried John away in the spirit into the wilderness. There he was shown a woman on a scarlet-colored beast, "full of names of blasphemy, having seven heads and ten horns" (v. 3). The woman herself was arrayed in scarlet-colored garments and decked with gold and precious stones. She had a golden cup in her hand "full of abominations and filthiness of her fornication" (v. 4). Upon her forehead a name was written: "MYSTERY, BABYLON THE GREAT, THE MOTHER OF HARLOTS AND ABOMINATIONS OF THE EARTH" (v. 5). She had been made drunk with the blood of the saints, the martyrs of Jesus. When John saw her he stood in amazement and wondered who she was.

This would have been enough to have identified the woman as a symbol of the wicked city of Rome, the citadel and seat of satanic reign. We have run across the name Babylon before and have observed that, for the first-century Christian, it no doubt referred to Rome. Because of the tight censorship John could not have used the word Rome; but just in case his readers did not pick up that clue, John goes on to give other clues which would surely remove all doubt or uncertainty.

This woman sits upon a beast which has seven heads and ten horns. At this point John urges his readers to use all of the wisdom which God has given them in order to decipher this code. It has to be couched in mystery in order to keep the Roman censors from intercepting it, but if they will use their heads wisely they can get the message.

From one point of view, John explains, the seven heads of the beast represent the seven mountains on which the woman sits. All who are familiar with Rome know that it is situated on seven hills. This was merely a means of identity. As if this were not enough, John goes on to explain that, looking at it from another point of view, the seven heads represent seven kings: "Five are fallen, and one is, and the other is not yet come; and when he cometh, he must continue a short space. And the beast that was, and is not, even he is the eighth, and is of the seven, and goeth into perdition" (vv. 10-11). This at first appears to be a senseless riddle, but it is not at all senseless when interpreted in the light of the known facts of history.

At the time John wrote, the eighth emperor was ruling over the mighty but wicked Roman Empire. In chronological order they were: Augustus (who

was on the throne at the time Jesus was born),
Tiberius, Caligula, Claudius, Nero, Vespasian, Ti-
tus, and Domitian. After the death of Nero three
men claimed the throne in rapid succession, but
none of the three lived long enough to establish
himself on the throne; therefore, they are not coun-
ted in the succession of the emperors, and they
were never considered by the people as emperors.
They were Galba (six months), Otho (four
months), and Vitellius (six months).

None of the eight mentioned above could be
classified as outstandingly good, but two of them
were notoriously bad: Nero and Domitian. There
grew up a popular legend among the people that
Nero did not really die and would return to the
throne again; or, if he had died, he would be rein-
carnated. When Domitian came along, he was so
much like Nero in disposition that many of the
people really believed that Domitian was the reincarnation of Nero. Of course, John and his fellow
Christians did not believe this legend; but John
did make use of it to identify the enemy. This is
the second time John has alluded to this legend
(see 13:3). Just why John positions himself in the
reign of Vespasian is not an easy question to answer. It could be another move designed to elude
the censors. However, if Domitian was the reincarnation of Nero, then he was in a sense the immediate successor of Nero, even though historically
this was Vespasian. John does explain that the
eighth king was also one of the seven. At any
rate, there is little reason to believe that these

first-century Christians did not understand what John was driving at in the riddle.

There are, of course, other interpretations of this riddle. For instance, Dr. W. A. Criswell, in his commentary on the Revelation, interprets these five fallen kings to refer to five ancient empires: Egyptian, Assyrian, Babylonian, Persian, and Greek.[1] The one that is refers to Rome, and the one that is yet to come is the "great, final, political dominion presided over by this anti-Christ, which is world government in its ultimate form." He goes on to explain that this final world government "will be divided into nations, into ten kingdoms"; and the ten kings of these ten kingdoms will give their power and strength to the Antichrist. William Hendriksen has a similar but slightly different interpretation.[2] He identifies the five empires as the Old Babylonian, the Assyrian, the New Babylonian, the Medo-Persian, and the Greco-Macedonian. The one that is he identifies with the Roman Empire, but he explains that the seventh "may stand for all anti-Christian governments between the fall of Rome and the final empire of antichrist." He suggests that since the eighth is "of the seven," the final kingdom of the Antichrist may very well arise in one of the ancient seats of Empire.

We certainly cannot afford to be dogmatic, but the interpretation which identifies these kings with the emperors of Rome, culminating with Domitian, seems to make much better sense. As we have said so many times throughout this study, for John and his first-century friends, the archenemy of God and God's redeemed people was the wicked and blasphemous empire of Rome. For those of us who live in the twentieth century, the principle may be applied to any similar godless regime. What John seeks to show here is that these blasphemous leaders and their wicked kingdoms will be utterly destroyed by the great power of the wrath of God in judgment. Just how complete this destruction is we shall see in the next scene.

Having clearly identified the enemy, John is ready to show us the utter devastation of the enemy territory—the great and wicked city, the center and citadel of wickedness. John saw a mighty angel swoop down out of heaven whose brilliance lighted the whole battlefield so that all could see. This angel cried with a loud voice, "Babylon the great is fallen, is fallen, and is become the habitation of devils, and the hold of every foul spirit, and a cage of every unclean and hateful bird" (18:2). Then in a vivid picture of contrast he shows the vast difference between the city's former glory and the dismal darkness of its present state. In her heyday Rome was lighted with brilliance. In her was gaiety, glamour, glitter, excitement, ostentation, and uninhibited licentiousness. She reigned like a queen, and all the nations gathered around her to offer homage and praise. People came from afar to profit by her worldwide trade marts and to enjoy her famous places of merriment.

But now look at her. She is desolate and forsaken. The men who lived deliciously by her stand afar off and mourn her downfall. It is as if a mighty

angel has taken her in his hand as one would
take a pebble from the beach and thumped it into
the sea. There is a brief ripple in the water and
then disappearance into oblivion. Thus has God
dealt with the wicked city. There is no more lucra-
tive trade within her, no more vivacious activities,
no more glamour. All is dull and dark. The utter
devastation is described by John in these dramatic
words: "And the voice of harpers, and musicians,
and of pipers, and trumpeters, shall be heard no
more at all in thee; and no craftsman, of whatsoever craft he be, shall be found any more in thee;
and the sound of a millstone shall be heard no
more at all in thee; / And the light of a candle
shall shine no more at all in thee; and the voice
of the bridegroom and of the bride shall be heard
no more at all in thee: for thy merchants were
great men of the earth; for by thy sorceries were
all nations deceived. / And in her was found the
blood of prophets, and of saints, and of all that
were slain upon the earth" (18:22-24).

Thus are we able to see how complete is God's
work of destruction on the satanic kingdom. The
saints of God will rejoice when they see it. This
picture of doom will find fulfillment in every great
city of this earth where satanic might has brought
on moral and spiritual corruption.

We turn from this picture of utter devastation,
which indeed is a part of the celebration, to look
at the more formal features of the celebration from
the heavenly side. This program of celebration in-
volves several very important events. The first to

come before our view in the apocalyptic vision is a heavenly concert by the heavenly choir. The third symbol in this series introduces us to the heavenly choir. After surveying the devastation in the territory of the wicked, John turns his face again toward heaven and hears "a great voice of much people." They are singing a song of victory. The introduction goes something like this: "Alleluia; Salvation, and glory, and honour, and power, unto the Lord our God" (19:1). The various sections of the heavenly choir, which will be composed of all the redeemed plus all of the angelic hosts of heaven, will come in for various refrains. The concert will begin with grandioso and work up to a climactic crescendo with these words: "Hallelujah: for the Lord God omnipotent reigneth." Handel's *The Messiah* will be nothing compared to this heavenly oratorio. Thus will we celebrate the victory with singing such as earth has never known.

The fourth feature of the celebration will be a great heavenly wedding. There is nothing here to indicate that John is attempting to give these events in proper chronological order. In fact, it makes little difference in what chronological order they may come. To get involved in chronology is to lose the true significance of these pictures. We only know that somewhere in the program of celebration there will be a beautiful wedding. The bridegroom is the Lamb himself, and the bride is a woman dressed in purest white, resplendent in glory. This woman is a symbol of the redeemed

who have been washed and made white in the
blood of the Lamb. These as one body constitute
the bride of Christ. These have been tested and
tried. They have come through triumphantly, and
now they are ready to be eternally united in a
heavenly ceremony with the victorious Lamb of
God. Now the saints are betrothed to Christ. At
the conclusion of the struggle we shall be united
with him in a heavenly and eternal wedding. There
will be a magnificent wedding supper, followed
by a procession and ceremony like this world has
never seen. We have seen some beautiful wed-
dings marked by splendor and grandeur, but none
will compare with the superlative splendor of this
heavenly wedding, the climax of a glorious victory
for the Lamb and his bride.

The fifth symbol in this series of celebrations
reveals a sumptuous and gigantic triumphal procession through the streets of heaven. John is so
entranced with what he sees that he falls down
at the feet of the angel who was showing him
these things. The angel rebukes him and reminds
him that only God is to be worshiped. John arises
to his feet and watches with keen interest the pag-
eantry which is set before him. Coming down the
main street of heaven John sees a white horse,
whose rider is called Faithful and True. His eyes
were as a flame of fire, and on his head were
many crowns. He was clothed with a vesture
dipped in blood, and he was also called the Word
of God. The term *word* or *logos* was one of John's
favorite expressions in referring to the Christ.

Across his vesture a title is written: "KING OF KINGS, AND LORD OF LORDS" (v. 16). There is no mistake. It is the Lamb of God, the captain of the victorious armies of the redeemed. Behind him follow a multitude of the redeemed. They also are riding white horses. It is a most impressive sight as we watch these armies of the Lord march by in their best dress, shouting, singing, and praising God.

This scene reminds us of another scene which took place nearly two thousand years ago. The Savior marched into Jerusalem for his triumphal entry. Then he rode on a lowly donkey and wore the humble rags of poverty. People gathered in the streets, some to slander him and a few to throw palm leaves in the path and shout, "Hosanna; Blessed is he that cometh in the name of the Lord" (Mark 11:9). What a contrast! Through John we see the real triumphal entry. The first was a mere shadow of the real thing. What ecstacy will be ours when we join in this heavenly procession through the streets of the New Jerusalem, following our triumphant Redeemer and Lord!

The sixth phase of the celebration will be the formal ceremony in which the earthly leaders of the wicked kingdom are given their official sentence. This is always an exciting time in the celebration of any victory. The leaders of the enemy, if not killed in battle, are immediately imprisoned; but later they are brought out and given an official sentence. We have already seen the utter destruction of the wicked empire city. Now John shows

us the tragic end of the wicked themselves, with
emphasis upon their earthly leaders—the first
beast and the second beast (the false prophet).
The birds of the heavens are seen to gather around
the carcasses of these dead enemies of the Lord
for a great feast. As we watch this ordeal we see
the old beast, the earthly leader of the wicked
empire, and his first assistant, the commune, as
they are taken and cast into a lake of fire burning
with brimstone. At the sight of this we can well
imagine that these persecuted Christians of Asia
Minor as they read this portion of the book burst
forth into a shout of praise, saying, "Hallelujah,
the Lord God omnipotent reigneth!"

In the interlude between the sixth and seventh
symbols we are privileged to see a very special
feature of the victory celebration. Many Bible
scholars have dulled or almost obscured this picture for the average reader by their endless de-
bates on one minor aspect of this phase of the
celebration—the reference to the thousand years
in the first six verses of the twentieth chapter.
We will not take the time or space here to elaborate on the many various facets of this debate
developed around the word *millennium,* a Latin
word which means a thousand years. The Greek
word as used in our text is *chilia.* The only other
time this word appears in the New Testament outside the Revelation is in 2 Peter 3:8. There Peter
simply mentioned the fact that "one day is with
the Lord as a thousand years, and a thousand
years as one day." There could be no possible

connection in any sense. It is an amazing thing that in this one brief passage we have the only reference to a millennium to be found in the Bible; yet volumes upon volumes have been written in an attempt to set out its apparent elaborate significance and meaning!

Whatever may be the significance of this reference to a thousand years, one thing is certain— the idea of a thousand years in this text is secondary and incidental, not primary. John certainly had no idea of setting out an elaborate doctrine of millennialism by his use of the term in this text. It is unfortunate that so many have become so engrossed in the theological technicalities of a millennial system of eschatology that they have become impervious to the blessedness of this aspect of God's redemptive program and victory celebration. It is incredible to think that men of no mean ability, realizing the symbolic nature of the book of Revelation and so interpreting many of the passages, will come to this particular passage and insist that it must be interpreted literally.

Following, then, what we believe to be a path of consistency, we interpret the "one thousand years" to mean an appreciable time, not necessarily a literal thousand years. Be that as it may, let us try to find the real significance of this total picture. The old dragon himself, the devil, is laid hold of by an angel, chained, and cast into the bottomless pit for a thousand years. During this thousand-year period, which John is privileged to see, the martyred dead are seen to reign with

Christ in a beautiful and glorious millennium. The actual duration of this thousand-year period is of minor consequence in the proper understanding of the true meaning of the text.

During this period, not all of the saints shall reign with Christ, as many have supposed—only the martyrs. The words of our text are very clear at this point. "And I saw thrones, and they sat upon them, and judgment was given unto them: and I saw the souls of them that were *beheaded* for the witness of Jesus, and for the word of God, and which had not worshipped the beast, neither his image, neither had received his mark upon their foreheads, or in their hands; and *they* lived and reigned with Christ a thousand years (20:4, author's italics).

Literally, this description would limit those who reigned with Christ to those martyred saints of the Domitian persecution. As we have said all along, John was thinking about those of his own generation; but the principle might well be applied to similar conditions of any generation. We are safe, therefore, in saying that during this period all the martyred saints shall reign with Christ.

The significance of the picture is simply this: Somewhere in God's economy and plan there will be a time and place in which God will give special recognition and tribute to those who have had to pay the supreme sacrifice of their lives for their faith in the Lord Jesus. This is exactly what we human beings are in the habit of doing. Every year in America on Memorial Day we pause as a nation to pay special tribute to those who have poured out their blood on the battlefields of this world in order that we might have the freedom and life which we now enjoy. This is nothing but right. To be sure, there are thousands of others who would have given their lives had they been called upon to do so; but since they were not called upon to do so, they are happy to join with all the citizens of our beloved nation in giving special tribute to those who did give their lives for their country. So far I have not been called upon to shed my blood for the cause of my Lord; and should I never be called upon to do so, I will gladly join the rest of the redeemed in taking a backseat, while those who have made the supreme sacrifice have a season of special tribute and honor.

It would appear from this passage that these martyred saints will be bodily resurrected from the dead for this special season of tribute before the other saints are so resurrected. John calls this "the first resurrection," and he tells us that the "rest of the dead lived not again until the thousand years were finished" (v. 5). This does not mean that the rest of the dead will not be alive or in existence during this period. It only means that they will not be alive in bodily form as will these martyrs during this period. At the end of this period the rest of the redeemed will also receive their resurrected bodies. What blessed comfort this must have been to those saints of Asia Minor who were constantly threatened with martyrdom, even as some of their fellow Christians had already suffered and had died for their faith!

This will be a glorious part of the victory celebration. It is nothing but right that God should
so honor his martyred saints. Exactly how long
this season will last is of minor consequence to
me. If it is literally a thousand years, even this
will be only a day in the light of eternity. Nor
am I able to discern all the details of this arrange-
ment, but the idea itself is sufficient to stir my
soul with ecstasy. Let us not miss the true meaning
of this part of the victory celebration by losing
ourselves in a maze of chronological details.

Now we are ready for the seventh symbol and
the climax of the celebration. The interlude has
given to us a picture of a special feature of the
celebration. Now we return to another aspect of
it in which all the redeemed participate. It, too,
has been quite a battleground of theological controversy. We are told that after this thousand-year
reign "Satan shall be loosed out of his prison, And
shall go out to deceive the nations which are in
the four quarters of the earth, Gog and Magog,
to gather them together to battle" (vv. 7-8). For
those who had been watching these pictures of
triumph, this scene perhaps comes as a shocking
surprise. According to the other scenes we had
supposed that the battle was over and that the
victory had already been celebrated. But now we
see the appearance of the old dragon going about
rallying recruits for a battle against the redeemed
of God. How can this be? After the matter is all
settled, does the battle break loose again? Is this

a reference to some future battle which will actually be fought? For those who insist on a literal interpretation, this could be the meaning; but once again let us try to see the idea or principle which John is trying to portray in this figurative picture.

This figure, like the others, is taken from the experiences of warfare. Rather than being another conflict as such, it is really a climactic part of the victory celebration. It was not at all uncommon in earlier days for the victors to celebrate their victory by bringing the captured leader of the enemy into their midst. In order to add to his chagrin, the victors give him a certain amount of liberty which is well circumscribed and guarded. In this apparent liberty the captured leader rants and raves while the people watch with glee. Before he is able to do any harm he is overtaken by those who stand on guard. Thus the victory is made all the more impressive. This is exactly what was done by the Philistines when they overcame the Israelites and captured their leader, Samson. As a part of their celebration they brought Samson out of his den where he had been blinded and placed him in their midst at a gala occasion in order to show how completely he had been subdued. Of course, they did not realize in this particular case that God would let him have a moment of resurging power in order to get vengeance for his people. But the idea is clear, and it was a very common practice in celebrating a victory.

The only other reference in the Bible to Gog and Magog is found in the thirty-eighth chapter

of Ezekiel. This reference by John is a commentary
on this Old Testament passage. One will have to
admit that this is a rather strange battle which
Ezekiel described in his vision. Israel is pictured
in peace and security with no attempt to defend
herself against the enemy who approaches. Without a struggle, as soon as the enemy arrives on
the scene, he is smitten with an awful judgment
directly from God. The rest of the vision tells of
a glorious celebration of victory on the part of
the people of Israel. In both passages the language
is highly figurative, and we must interpret it as
such. If this is the meaning of John's reference
to Gog and Magog, it is also the meaning of Ezekiel's reference to it; at least, this is the way John
interpreted it since he uses the same symbolic language. The only difference is that John's version
is a little more complete and is given to us in
the fuller light of the New Testament revelation.
In both instances the struggle is already over, and
the people of God are settled down in security
and peace. There is no struggle at all; and before
any damage is done to the people of God, an awful
judgment from God falls upon these forces of evil.

This, it seems to me, is exactly what John is
depicting in this last symbol of victory. The victorious redeemed are gathered together on Mount
Zion for the last phase of their victory celebration.
The old devil is brought out of his pit where he
had been placed. He is turned loose in their midst
to rant and to rave, thinking that he is free to
wage war against the redeemed of God. He gathers

up his forces; but before he is able to harm a hair on the head of one saint, "fire came down from God out of heaven, and devoured them" (v. 9). There is no actual conflict. The redeemed watch with shouts of ecstasy as the old devil is cast into the lake of fire and brimstone to take his place in torment along with the beast and the false prophet. This is the climax of a most magnificent celebration of victory. We are almost breathless as we watch with John the victorious consummation of this sublime program of celebration. Only one thing now remains. We must see the permanent state of being after the celebration is over. This will be the subject of our last episode in the drama of redemption.

CHAPTER TEN

The Eternal State
(20:10 to 22:5)

We have come now to the last of the seven acts in the drama of redemption as revealed to John the apostle through that open door into heaven. You will recall that when the first scene opened in the first verse of the fourth chapter, we saw with John a majestic throne on which sat a sovereign God. As the curtain opens for this last scene, we see this same white throne with this same sovereign God sitting upon it. We are back where we started.

But there is one striking difference between the first and the last scene. In the first scene we saw a scroll rolled up and sealed in the hand of him who sat upon this throne. In the last scene we see the same sovereign God, but the scroll is gone. This scroll symbolized the judgments of a righteous God. These have been executed by the Lamb. These judgments were described; then we saw the angels of warning as they sounded their trumpets to warn all men of these impending judgments. The wicked of the world would not heed the warnings, and the result was a terrific conflict between the forces of evil in the world and the forces of righteousness represented by God's own redeemed people. We saw this conflict in all of its fury and then the frightful climax as God poured out his seven bowls of wrath. Following this climax of the battle we were privileged with John to get a preview of the celebration which shall take place among the redeemed of God in glory when this struggle shall have been consummated.

Only one thing remains to be understood in this unfolding story of redemption. After the celebration is over, what about the permanent state of existence for the redeemed as well as the unredeemed? Our last episode answers this question. In this vision we are given a brief glimpse of the state of the unredeemed and a much longer glimpse of the state of the redeemed. Since there are only two possible destinies for all mankind, this last episode in our drama has only two subdivisions instead of the seven which appeared in all of the other episodes.

It was not necessary or expedient to dwell at length on the destiny of the wicked; therefore, John gives only six verses to this as opposed to thirty-one verses to the destiny of the redeemed. Through John God gives us just enough to let us know that the defeat of the wicked is thorough, permanent, and eternal. As the curtain rises we see the peoples of the earth, small and great, stand before that throne to receive the recompense of their eternal reward. For the unbeliever it is a dreadful day. The books are opened in which an accurate and complete account has been kept of every deed, thought, and disposition. According to that book all men stand condemned before the judgment throne.

But there is another book that shall be opened before the judgment throne. It is the book of life— that is, the Lamb's book of life. In it are written the names of those who have received the Lamb and his atoning blood. By the first book we shall all be judged and consigned unto an eternal torment, but those whose names are written in the Lamb's book of life will be welcomed into the portals of a glorious eternity. The only hope, therefore, for a happy eternity is based upon our reception of the blood of Jesus as our atonement and not upon any accomplishments of our own in moral living. It behooves every one of us, therefore, to see that his name is written in the Lamb's book of life. The beloved hymn writer B. B. McKinney has expressed it for us in these beautiful words:

> I am bought not with riches,
>   Neither silver nor gold;
> But Christ hath redeemed me,
>   I am safe in His fold;
> In the Book of his kingdom
>   With its pages so fair;
> Through Jesus my Saviour,
>   My name's written there.
>
> Oh! that beautiful city,
>   With its mansions of light,
> With its glorified beings,
>   In pure garments of white;
> Where no evil thing cometh

> To despoil what is fair;
> Where the angels are watching,
> My name's written there.[1]

In describing the eternal fate of the unbeliever, John uses three significant analogies: the bottomless pit, the lake of fire, and the second death. There is no human language that we can use to describe what a godless eternity will be like, but these three expressions give us a faint idea. The old dragon was cast into the abyss, the bottomless pit (20:3). Those whose names were not found written in the Lamb's book of life were cast into the lake of fire (20:15). Even after he had introduced the first picture of the destiny of the redeemed, John comes back once more (21:8) to show by way of contrast the awful destiny of the unbelievers who "shall have their part in the lake which burneth with fire and brimstone." Then John goes on to explain that this is the same as the "second death" (20:14). It is a fearful and horrible sight.

If someone should remind us that this is only a figurative picture and not a real picture of hell, we must answer by saying that if this is a figurative picture—and we believe that it is—the real thing which it symbolizes must be actually worse than the figure itself. Call it by any name you please, hell will be the sensation of always falling but never arriving at the bottom; always burning but never becoming extinct; always dying but never dead. Such a condition awaits all those who refuse the pardoning grace of Christ which was made possible by his atoning death on Calvary.

We hasten to turn our eyes from this dreadful sight to the blessed picture of the destiny of the redeemed. Those whose names are written down in the Lamb's book of life are issued into a life which is inexplicably and inextricably glorious. This life is described by John (that is, as far as human language can describe it) in three figures or symbols, each one accentuating a certain aspect of this blessed life.

In the first symbol heaven is pictured to us as a large tabernacle. It is full of happy people who are singing praises to him who sits in the midst of this tabernacle, God. What a blessed privilege to sit at the feet of our God and of his Christ and to praise and adore him through eternity. Heaven will be a place of happy worship. We wonder what some people will do when they get to heaven, if indeed they do get there as they claim they shall. These people find it a grievous ordeal to come to the house of the Lord for worship once a month or once a year. Surely these will feel somewhat out of place if they do get to heaven, where we will worship the Lord in the beauty of holiness through eternity! I am persuaded to believe that the author of the old spiritual was about right when he said, "Everybody talkin' about heaven ain't goin' there!"

To be sure, there will be no more long-winded and dry sermons. Neither will there be any more appeals to unsaved souls; but there will be plenty of singing, shouting, and testifying to the glory and praise of our everlasting Savior. Heaven will be a place humming with activity. We will be busy in the worship activities of our King throughout eternity. The difference between then and now will be that this heavenly activity will never leave us fatigued, exhausted, or in pain. "And God shall wipe away all tears from their eyes; and there shall be no more death, neither sorrow, nor crying, neither shall there be any more pain; for the former things are passed away" (21:4).

Our second symbol of heaven is in the form of a beautiful and majestic city. One of the angels who held the seven bowls of wrath invites John to come with him so that he might show him "that great city, the holy Jerusalem, descending out of heaven from God, Having the glory of God" (21:10-11). John is carried to a high mountain, where he sees this heavenly city. For the Oriental of John's day a city was a symbol of protection and convenience. Most cities were walled and therefore protected from the outside. In using this symbol, God seems to be magnifying the protective as well as the beautiful aspect of heaven. The city lies four square bounded by high walls with three gates on each side made of pearl. There are twelve foundations made of precious stones. The streets are paved with gold. It is full of light, glory, and beauty. Let us keep in mind that this is a figurative picture. The real heaven which it symbolizes will far exceed in glory the image which we are able to see through our finite minds and to express through our inadequate language.

If you can imagine one of our great modern cities with its beautiful homes, lovely boulevards, inspiring parks, and modern conveniences and without its slum areas, sinful roadhouses, glaring liquor signs, hospitals, and funeral homes, you might have a faint idea of what heaven is like. There will be no need of artificial light, for God himself will provide the light. There will be no dreary nights. The glory of the nations will be brought into it; and, best of all, there will be no sin in it. "And there shall in no wise enter into it anything that defileth, neither whatsoever worketh abomination, or maketh a lie, but they which are written in the Lamb's book of life" (21:27). The thing that always mars the beauty of our earthly cities is the sin which is so predominant in them. It is difficult to appreciate the beauty of our modern cities when we think of all the unholy activity and satanic designs which are so frequently encountered. A glorious and majestic city without sin, pain, and corruption—that is heaven!

The third symbol of heaven comes to us in the form of a garden. The picture is so exquisite we must quote John's description of it. "And he shewed me a pure river of water of life, clear as crystal, proceeding out of the throne of God and of the Lamb. / In the midst of the street of it, and on either side of the river, was there the tree of life, which bare twelve manner of fruits, and yielded her fruit every month: and the leaves of the tree were for the healing of the nations. / And there shall be no more curse; but the throne of

God and of the Lamb shall be in it; and his servants shall serve him: / And they shall see his face; and his name shall be in their foreheads. / And there shall be no night there; and they need no candle, neither light of the sun; for the Lord God giveth them light; and they shall reign for ever and ever" (22:1-5).

The Bible begins with a garden and closes with a garden. What a testimony to the symmetry and unity of the Bible! The Bible opens with a beautiful garden, the Garden of Eden; but soon the beauty fades away with the coming of disobedience and sin. Man was driven from the garden to work by the sweat of his brow amidst thorns and thistles. We are told that the tree of life in the midst of the garden was protected by a cordon of cherubim and flaming swords. We travel on through the Bible in the maze of sin, watching men as they fall prey to the power of sin, until we come upon another garden. It is the garden of Gethsemane. In this garden Jesus won the victory which made possible this last garden of glory. In the Garden of Eden the word was "my will, not thine, be done"; in the garden of Gethsemane it was "thy will, not mine, be done." In this was conquered the power of sin and Satan. Thus the way was opened which led back to the garden of God all of those who exercise faith in the Savior who won the victory in the garden of Gethsemane.

So we return to the garden. The thorns and thistles are gone. The tree of life has been kept in the midst of the garden and is now made available

to all of those who have found their way into this
garden through the blood of the Lamb. What a
blessed picture of peace and tranquillity! The pure
river of water of life runs through the midst of
it, never running dry. The tree of life bears fruit
every month throughout the year for the suste-
nance of the people. The leaves of the tree ensure
good health. What more could one want? The first
garden was once fair and beautiful, but there came
a curse. In this garden "there shall be no more
curse" (v. 3). Alleluia! The throne of God and of
the Lamb will be in the midst of the garden, and
we shall see him face to face. In this beautiful
garden the redeemed of the Lamb shall reign with
him forever and forever. Alleluia!

Now let us close our eyes and try for a moment
to envision this whole thing. Let us imagine that
there is a small group of Christians who have as-
sembled in the home of one of the members in
the little town of Smyrna. The curtains are drawn
for fear of the Roman persecutors. The people
scarcely raise their voices for fear of being heard
by some spy. These Christians are despondent and
weary, their hope almost gone. They wonder if
there is any encouragement for the future. To them
the future is very dark and foreboding. Some of
their loved ones have already been caught in the
great net of Roman persecution. Who will be next?
Their beloved preacher and pastor has been taken
off to some lonely isle and many have been killed
for all they knew. Could they hold on much longer?

As they are praying, a knock is heard at the

door. Their hearts leap within them, and they jump
with fear. Surely it must be some officer of the
law coming to inflict more punishment upon these
rebellious citizens who refuse to bow down before
the image of the emperor. When the door is
opened, they are pleasantly surprised to see a fellow believer from Ephesus. He holds in his hands
a scroll. Quickly he tells them the news that he
has come to bring them a message from their aged
pastor and fellow-sufferer who was still living on
the Isle of Patmos. Eagerly and with pent-up emotions they listen as the reader opens the scroll
and begins to read.

They seem to lose all sense of time and place
as they find themselves with John, looking through
that open door into heaven. Into the night they
read with no thought of exhaustion. Their hearts
begin to tingle as they see the great white throne
and the unfolding of this redemptive story. Their
tears of sorrow turn to tears of joy as they see
the judgments of God expressed against their godless persecutors. Now and then someone forgets
where he is and shouts out a lusty "Alleluia."
What a thrill it would have been could we have
been peeping through a crack in the curtains to
watch the faces of these once-bewildered Christians! As they watch the bowls of God's wrath
emptied out upon the godless beast and his cohorts, they involuntarily find themselves joining
in with the heavenly choir as they sing forth
praises to their God.

When the beast and the false prophet are cast

into the lake of fire, the believers' hearts leap with joy. Then when they see the heavenly wedding and the triumphal procession, they cannot contain themselves. That scene which reveals the special recognition which God has planned for his martyred saints brings blessed comfort. And then with sweet peace and tranquillity of soul they listen as the reader takes them to the heavenly city and the beautiful garden. When the reader has finished the description of the blessed garden, they burst forth into a doxology of praise, not caring how many Roman spies may have been lurking outside. After the doxology they fall on their knees in prayer, thanking God for his wonderful redemption and pledging themselves afresh to be faithful and loyal to him in the battle until the day is done and the victory is won. They leave their meeting place with this song in their hearts: "The kingdoms of this world are become the kingdoms of our Lord, and of his Christ; and he shall reign for ever and ever, king of kings and lord of lords. Amen and Alleluia! the Lord God omnipotent reigneth!"

I find the same emotions stirring in my own soul as I finish looking with John at this panoramic picture of redemption. Do you not also feel the same? Let us, therefore, go forth with renewed courage and zeal to be faithful to our Lord and his commission, even unto death.

Notes

PREFACE

1. H. E. Dana, *The Epistles and Apocalypse of John* (Dallas: Baptist Book Store, 1937).

CHAPTER 1

1. W. A. Criswell, *Expository Sermons on Revelation,* vol. 1 (Grand Rapids: Zondervan Publishing House, 1962), p. 14.

2. A. M. Hunter, *Introducing the New Testament* (Philadelphia: The Westminster Press, 1957), p. 188.

3. Albert Barnes, *Notes on the Book of Revelation* (New York: Harper & Brothers, 1864).

4. B. H. Carroll, *An Interpretation of the English Bible* (New York: Fleming H. Revell Company, 1913).

5. C. I. Scofield, *Holy Bible.* (Reference Edition.)

6. George E. Ladd, *Crucial Questions About the Kingdom of God* (Grand Rapids: William B. Eerdmans Publishing Company, 1952).

7. Criswell, vol. 1, p. 14.

8. J. Dwight Pentecost, *Prophecy for Today* (Grand Rapids: Zondervan Publishing House, 1961).

9. John F. Walvoord, *The Millennial Kingdom* (Grand Rapids: Zondervan Publishing House, 1959).

10. Albertus Pieters, *The Lamb, the Woman, and the Dragon* (Grand Rapids: Zondervan Publishing House, 1937).

11. J. Gresham Machen, *Christianity and Liberalism*

(Grand Rapids: William B. Eerdmans Publishing Company, 1923).

12. Dana.

13. Ray Summers, *Worthy Is the Lamb* (Nashville: Broadman Press, 1951).

14. David Freeman, *The Bible and Things to Come* (Grand Rapids: Zondervan Publishing House, 1939).

15. Pieters.

CHAPTER 2

1. Summers, p. 5.

2. Walvoord, p. 65.

3. Floyd E. Hamilton, *The Basis of Millennial Faith* (Grand Rapids: William B. Eerdmans Publishing Company, 1942), pp. 53-54.

4. Criswell, vol. 1, p. 81.

5. Criswell, vol. 3, p. 57.

6. W. Hendriksen, *More Than Conquerors* (Grand Rapids: Baker Book House, 1947), pp. 23-31.

7. Carroll.

8. Criswell, vol. 1, pp. 173-184.

CHAPTER 5

1. R. C. H. Lenski, *The Interpretation of St. John's Revelation* (Columbus, Ohio: The Wartburg Press, 1943), p. 222.

2. Criswell, vol. 3, pp. 90-98.

3. J. B. Lawrence, *A New Heaven and a New Earth* (New York: The American Press, 1960), pp. 53-57.

4. Dana, p. 119.

5. Summers, p. 139.

6. Albert H. Baldinger, *Preaching from Revelation* (Grand Rapids: Zondervan Publishing House, 1960), pp. 31-34.

CHAPTER 6

1. Charles John Ellicott, *Ellicott's Bible Commentary* (Grand Rapids: Zondervan Publishing House, 1939).

2. Albert Barnes, *Notes, Explanatory and Practical, on the Book of Revelation* (New York: Harper & Brothers, 1851).

3. Philip Mauro, *Patmos Visions* (Boston: Hamilton, 1925).

4. Justin A. Smith, *Commentary on the Revelation* (Philadelphia: American Baptist Publication Society, 1883).

5. Leon Morris, *The Revelation of St. John* (Grand Rapids: William B. Eerdmans, 1969), p. 122.

6. Edward Gibbon, *The Decline and Fall of the Roman Empire* (New York: Dell Publishing Company, 1963).

CHAPTER 7

1. Henry Barclay Swete, *The Apocalypse of St. John* (New York: Macmillan Company, 1906).

2. Lenski, p. 222.

3. Morris, p. 122.

CHAPTER 8

1. Hendriksen, p. 196.

2. Baldinger, p. 94.

CHAPTER 9

1. Criswell, vol. 5.

2. Hendriksen, pp. 200-206.

CHAPTER 10

1. Words by B. B. McKinney and M. A. Kidder, 1940. Copyright © 1940 by Broadman Press, Nashville, Tennessee. Used by permission.